Paw Prints

from the creators of 'The Printmaker's Cat'

Rembrandt van Rijn (1606–1669) was a printmaking legend and an early exponent of the etching process. Mychael Barratt here uses the Japanese gampi (tea-stained) paper favoured by the Dutch master to print his own imaginative etching, 'Rembrandt's Dog' – "an attempt to picture what kind of dog Rembrandt would have had"

MADE IN NORFOLK BY MASCOT MEDIA

Published in Great Britain in 2019 by
Mascot Media, Norfolk, UK.
Email: mascot_media@btinternet.com
www.mascotmedia.co.uk

A CIP catalogue record for this book is available from
the British Library.

ISBN: 978-1-9164783-5-0

Written and designed by Alan Marshall, with editorial
contributions from artists. Edited by Marion Scott Marshall.

Printed by Swallowtail Print, Drayton Industrial Park,
Taverham Road, Drayton, Norwich, Norfolk NR8 6RL.
Email: contact@swallowtailprint.co.uk
www.swallowtailprint.co.uk

The publishers beg the forgiveness of their cats...

CAPTIONS. *Front cover artists, top row from left: Alison Read; Helen Fay; Guy Allen; Hazel McNab. Middle row from left: Neil Bousfield; Sonia Rollo; Tor Hildyard; Chris Sinden; Katharine Green; Sarah Bays. Bottom row from left: Nick Wonham; Mary Collett; Pat Schaverien; Andy English. Front cover flap: Sarah Cemmick. Back cover artists, top row from left: Mychael Barratt; Gill Munn; Anna Tosney; Marian Carter. Row 2 from left: Andrew Stock; Ruth Green; Geri Waddington; Chris Sinden. Row 3 from left: Jane Constable; Chris Daunt; Emily Smith Polyblank; Ian Mowforth. Bottom row from left: Amie Haslen; Jackie Curtis; Hannah Firmin; Hilary Paynter.*

To Flush, My Dog ~ Elizabeth Barrett Browning

*'Underneath my stroking hand,
Startled eyes of hazel bland
Kindling, growing larger,
Up thou leapest with a spring,
Full of prank and curveting,
Leaping like a charger.'*

Left: Freedom (vinyl cut) ~ Nick Wonham

Below: Hokusai's Dog by Mychael Barratt *"This piece was inspired by a visit to a Hokusai exhibition at the British Museum. It was an ordeal just to get into the building let alone look at the work, but standing in front of his famous woodcut made it all worthwhile. I've tried to be true to the drama and the majesty of the original; but, hopefully, the eagerness and excitement of the dog and the warmer palette create the impression that everything is going to be okay."*

Contents

Artists from top to bottom: Alison Read; Hazel McNab; Ian Mowforth; Nick Wonham

Every dog must

The inclusion of dogs in art is hardly a new phenomenon. Ever since they first befriended mankind, they have been recorded as working animals, pets or simply aesthetically pleasing objects. The remains of the ancient Roman city of Pompeii yielded a dog mosaic. The volcanic eruption in AD 79 may have buried the owner's home, but it could well have been standing a hundred years earlier, implying that artists were portraying household dogs long before Vesuvius struck.

Marble statues of Greyhound-like dogs have also been found dating back to the first century AD, demonstrating the longevity of both the breed and the art form. As the Renaissance delivered its onslaught of cultural creativity, dogs began to appear more frequently as companions rather than just workers. Smaller, more decorative breeds started to feature in paintings, supplementing the usual elegant hunting hounds.

Venice in the 16th century was seemingly awash with dog-adorned images. Jacopo Bassano took the art form to a new level and made a very nice living from painting dogs. Cesare Ripa's *Iconologia* from 1593 suggests that "the dog is the most faithful animal in the world, and beloved by men". This, combined with their indications of high social status, meant wealthy Venetians built big houses and filled them with big dogs – as well as big paintings of big dogs.

While the cat in art has tended to be frowned upon by the establishment, reflecting its (disputed) lower status in the household, there is barely a name on the honour roll of painters that isn't associated with at least one canine-inspired

Debbie Kendall and Figo share some studio time

masterpiece. Rembrandt, Dürer, Renoir, Degas, Goya, Singer Sargent, Manet, Stubbs, Gainsborough, Landseer, Gaugin, Rossetti, Marc and Munch share the wall space with Picasso, Rockwell, Warhol, Kahlo, Hockney and Freud. Even Jeff Koons has dabbled in 3D dog art.

All of this suggests that this book, with its focus entirely on contemporary printmaking, has been too long in the making. Given that *The Printmaker's Cat* first appeared in July 2013 and has seen a revised version and additional printings since then, we can be accused of having neglected man's best friend. Virtually every day since the ink dried on the pages of our first multi-artist printmaking book, people have been asking when the dog version would appear.

Like many surprisingly successful books, *The Printmaker's Cat* was unplanned. We had no idea if the British public's fondness for felines would translate into demand for a collection of linocuts, etchings, screenprints, wood engravings, collagraphs and woodcuts by 20th-century artists. That book came about because we noticed that a great number of printmakers enjoyed

have his day...

the company of cats and repaid them by putting images of them on to paper.

At the time, dogs were largely absent from the scene. Our studio visits seldom resulted in canine encounters. The relative lack of self-sufficiency exhibited by dogs and the consequent need for companionship, walks and regular feeding makes for a different kind of relationship.

Cats can snooze in sunny corners of the studio or print room, heading off for solitary excursions when it suits them. Dogs, even the smaller breeds, are seldom left to their own devices where tubes of ink, piles of tempting paper and drying prints can be found. In short, we convinced ourselves that printmaking and dog ownership were somewhat incompatible.

Perhaps we were wrong, or maybe things have changed during the past six years. We had 'tested the water' on a few occasions, as some of the patient artists here can verify. We would float the idea of a 'Printmaker's Dog' type of title, and then abandon it thanks to a mixed response or a limited quantity of suitable material. All the time, however, dog lovers and book retailers kept reminding us that we were potentially

missing out on a great opportunity.

The multi-artist concept has now taken us from cats, via the extraordinary success of *The Artful Hare* through chickens, owls, gardens and, most recently, water birds. The time had surely come to take our canine chums seriously. After all, according to Jonathan Swift, 'Every dog must have his day'. This volume, sporting a hopefully catchy title, *Paw Prints*, will establish whether a diverse portfolio of dog images will prove

Kessie minding the press in the studio of Max Angus

as popular as its cat-themed predecessor.

Part of the charm of *The Printmaker's Cat* was the link between the featured creatures and their keepers. The stories were often sad, reflecting pets lost along the way, but sometimes funny and always heart-warming. We have sought to capture some of the same spirit here. While not every dog is owned by, or even known by, the artist in question, the majority are – and so the accompanying text is often of a personal nature.

We were worried by breed preference. With the majority of cats, they are simply cats. Even the pedigree varieties have characteristics very much in common with those of their moggy cousins. With dogs, however, some people will only ever share their homes and lives with one breed, providing a form of 'brand loyalty' that is perhaps unique to this area of pet ownership.

Some of these breeds go back many generations and often represent the working dogs of the past. We expected retrievers, spaniels, lurchers and sheepdogs to proliferate. However, recent years have seen some flavours of dog become fashion statements, and others created by deliberate cross-fertilisation. In stark contrast, some traditional dog types appear to be on the brink of extinction, so far out of favour have they fallen.

So-called 'toy' varieties have always been popular, adorning oil paintings by the great masters as these miniature beasts sit as patiently as the owner under the artist's unforgiving gaze. Perhaps these more manageable miniatures are more suited to studio life than their larger brethren, who demand more exercise, attention and food.

The biggest gamble we have therefore taken with *Paw Prints* is to mix and match more than 50 varieties of dog breed without any attempt to organise. There is no simple way of seeking out Scotties, winkling out Whippets or pinpointing Pointers.

Our second big risk is that, as usual, we opened the book up to as many artists as possible (exactly 76) and achieved the desired wide variation in styles. Highly experienced dog 'experts' rub shoulders with less well-established printmakers who merely dabble with the occasional canine subject. There are artists here who normally devote their talents to birds or flora, but such is their love for a hairy companion that dog prints have joined the portfolio.

Detailed and highly realistic depictions such as those by Helen Fay and Guy Allen share space with more whimsical interpretations, including those of Alison Read, Helen D Moore, Lucy Gell and Ruth Green. Mychael Barratt even lent us some of his inspired 'artists and dogs' series, with his Rembrandt-based etching gracing the title page. We wanted to showcase as big a cross-section of the printmaker's art as possible, so that there should be something for everyone.

Please forgive us, dog lovers, if this collection is entirely too random and tricky to navigate. The images are ordered simply by contributing artist – and even those aren't in alphabetical sequence. It is as if we have made it as difficult as possible to spot your favourite (perhaps a Dalmatian?).

This, of course, is the essence of the 'coffee table' book. While our modest volume will nestle comfortably on the arm of a chair or any smaller surface, the book is very much designed for frequent visits rather than a cover-to-cover read in one sitting. There is absolutely no useful information about breeds, description of characteristics or even tips on feeding, training or behaviour.

We hope that the dogs will speak for themselves, at least in the sense that the portraits will often provide more than a glimpse of the individual's character. Some dogs are more metaphors than accurate representations. They may on occasion have been included just to add extra interest to a scene – although we've avoided a lot of the 'lurcher in landscape' type of illustration.

An exception had to be made for gifted wood engraver Neil Bousfield, living on the north-east coast of Norfolk and producing original and greatly admired prints that

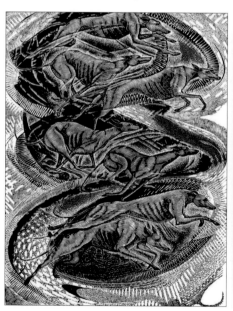

combine his love of the changing and ever-threatened local landscape with the sleek greyhound shapes of his Whippets.

Not every breed of dog popular in the UK will appear on these pages, although we have turned no species away. This is simply a reflection of what the printmakers have made. The canine population reflects dogs from artists' households, pet portrait commissions and sometimes random reproductions of a passing pooch that caught the printmaker's eye.

It was probably clear from the title of *The Printmaker's Cat* that all of the artwork came in the form of so-called 'original prints'. The images were editioned ink-based prints on paper originating from carved blocks, etched plates, etc. The joy of that collection was the ability of so many different artists to use several well-established techniques to interpret the animals in myriad ways.

This collection has an identical aim

and, once again, you will find no paintings, drawings or sculptures here – except for the occasional working sketch from which the resulting print was made. For those of you rather more familiar with dogs than with printmaking, this portfolio should impress and entertain. You will learn a little (or perhaps quite a lot) about the processes used, with a glossary of terms on page 10.

Printmaking at the more populist level is undergoing a renaissance. The materials can be affordable, the space required can be modest and the results achieved even early on the experience curve can be gratifyingly good. The resulting art, sold in small editions of slightly varying hand-made prints, will generally be affordable.

While the 'fine art' extreme of the spectrum may still be dominated by paintings, bronzes and sculpture, printmaking has always had its place. There are some highly skilled artists working in other media who still turn their hand to

printmaking, where the ability to capture an image is combined with the practical skills of cutting, scraping, inking and pressing to deliver spectacular results.

Artists contributing to this book may take the opportunity to explain their love of the processes used, the subjects themselves, and why dogs represent both a challenge and a reward when selected to become the basis for an edition.

Take Ely-based wood engraver Andy English, for example. "Of all the creatures I have made engravings of, it seems to me that my images of dogs are always portraits. There is always a definite personality to be captured and the setting is always important, whether interior or exterior.

From left to right: Runners (wood engraving) – Neil Bousfield. Brenda (linocut) – Ian Mowforth. Who's the Guilty One? (drypoint/monoprint) – Anna Tosney. Envy 1 (collagraph) – Mary Collett. Beachcombing (linocut) – Hilke MacIntyre. Like a Dance (woodcut) – Emily Smith Polyblank.

Some of my wood engravings have cats passing through or lingering in a warm spot. However, the dogs are more likely to occupy or even seem to own their place."

Debbie Kendall's dog-based compositions are among the more unusual and eye-catching in this collection, as she eschews the traditional dog portrait for something quite thought-provoking. "I hand-print art for people who love dogs, inspired by my muse and companion, a Portuguese Water Dog named Figo. I use hand-lettered words and illustration to interpret the unique connection people have with their dogs. I do a lot of 'dog watching' – observing how dogs react and adapt to life in a human world is a constant source of interest to me. I am continually heartened, encouraged and honoured to produce work that dog lovers can identify with."

Printmaking techniques, which can often provide a depth or texture absent in other forms of two-dimensional art, do lend themselves to animals such as dogs, as evidenced by Ian Mowforth's comments. "It is important that the material can represent the physical quality of the dog's coat, and lino is entirely appropriate for this. I choose the subjects due to their physical presence. My goal is to capture the life of the dog as the image will outlive the dog."

Janet Gardner has also found the texture and depth of image possible in print inspiring, and believes it has allowed her to explore the way she can capture and express the character of a dog. Our canine friends particularly inspire Guy Allen – he delights in the technical skill required to capture dogs' musculature and movement.

Printmaker Mary Collett is very specific as regards the element of a dog that she seeks to perfect. "Big wet noses are one of the best bits of a dog, so I wanted to do some small prints that emphasised the nose – hence my Little Big Nosed Dogs. I hate tracing so I work by just drawing straight on to the lino in pastel or chalk to indicate the light and dark areas of the print and any features I want to emphasise (the eyes!). This then gives me the freedom to cut the area in a lively way and gives the image more life."

Tor Hildyard champions the use of a different printmaking medium for dogs and other creatures. "I find collagraphs are a wonderful medium for expressing exciting marks and textures when it comes to making prints of animals. The tearing and collaging of small pieces of paper, alongside the layering of different glues and pastes as well as the mistakes that turn into glorious unforeseen textures, all add to this understated medium." 🐾

Opposite: Dog Show (wood engraving) – Hilary Paynter (see page 15). Below left: Stanley (screenprint) – Ruth Green (see page 52). Below centre: Gormley's Dog (etching) – Mychael Barratt (see page 12): "This etching was designed to resemble one of Antony Gormley's figurative wire sculptures as a dog". Bottom right: Winnie, sitting (linocut) – Roz Howling (see page 78).

PRINTMAKING GLOSSARY

Background image courtesy of Debbie Kendall

Original print: an image created from hand-cut or hand-drawn printing blocks, plates or stencils that are used to produce a limited number of prints, usually numbered and signed by the artist.

Relief print: made by cutting the image out of a flat surface, usually wood or lino. The remaining raised areas then form the relief block to which ink is applied by means of a roller.

Intaglio print: made by cutting into a flat surface by hand, as in engraving, or by using acid to burn into a metal plate, as in etching. The depth and density of the pits and hollows control the tone of the finished print.

Wood engraving: the image is cut with sharp tools into the end grain of a block of wood, usually box or lemonwood, in which very fine detailed work can be engraved.

Woodcut (also woodblock): the design is worked into the side grain or plank of the wood with the cutting generally following the direction of the grain. The grain itself can be incorporated into the design.

Linocut: the surface material is cut away from hessian-backed linoleum, a relatively soft material that can be mounted on to wood to give extra support. Multiple colours can be achieved by cutting multiple blocks of lino, or by inking, continuing to cut away and re-inking the same block (the reduction or reductive method). Vinyl can be used as an alternative to lino.

Etching: a flat metal plate (copper, zinc, steel) is first coated with an acid-resistant ground. The design is scratched through the hardened coating, exposing the metal below. The whole plate is then immersed in acid that burns or etches only the exposed areas of the metal plate where the design has been drawn.

Aquatint: a process used to etch large areas of even tone. A fine, even layer of acid-resistant powdered resin is dusted over the surface of the plate. When the plate is heated, the resin melts and fixes to the plate. The design is painted out with acid-resistant varnish. The acid bites into the metal plate between the individual grains of resin.

Drypoint: a sharp-pointed steel tool is used to inscribe directly into the surface of a metal or perspex plate. Not only is a line inscribed into the surface but a burr is pushed up that holds the ink and prints as a thick, velvety line.

Mezzotint: using a rocker – a flat steel blade with a fine serrated edge – thousands of tiny indented holes are made evenly over the entire surface of a copper plate. This will print as an even, rich, velvety black.

Screenprint (also serigraph and silkscreen): a fine woven mesh (originally silk, but today synthetic) is stretched tightly over a frame. Stencils are used to mask out the areas of the screen that are not to be printed. A sheet of paper is laid under the screen, then a flat rubber blade is drawn over it, forcing ink through the open areas not masked by the stencils.

Collagraph: a print made from a collaged or textured board. One method is to work in relief, applying a variety of materials on to the surface of a cardboard plate. Another approach is an intaglio method achieved by scoring lines into the surface and cutting away layers of card with a scalpel, thereby creating recesses that will hold ink.

Lithograph: a design is drawn or painted directly on to a prepared surface, originally limestone and today more usually zinc or aluminium. Once the image is drawn, the surface undergoes a chemical process, making the undrawn areas sensitive to water. The drawn areas remain sensitive to oil-based ink. During the printing process, the 'stone' is constantly dampened and the surface is inked up with a roller. The ink adheres to the greased areas and is repelled by the areas that are wet.

Monoprint/monotype: both are one-off print techniques in which an image, produced on a metal plate, sheet of glass or any other flat surface, is transferred to paper. There are two basic methods of working. In the subtractive approach, a metal plate or sheet of glass is inked up by means of a roller, and the image is produced by selectively wiping away the ink. In the additive approach, ink, paint or water-based media can be painted directly on to the plate. These methods can be used in combination with other print techniques.

Mixed media: a work produced using two or more printing processes.

Solarplate™ etching (also photopolymer plate): a light-sensitive metal plate is etched through the action of ultraviolet light. An opaque image on transparent film is placed on the prepared plate, then exposed to light before plain water is used to 'fix' the image before inking and printing.

Richmond Park, Winter (after Bruegel) – Mychael Barratt
(see overleaf). Etching inspired by a trip to Vienna to see a
retrospective of the work of Pieter Bruegel the Elder. Mychael's
Dachshund Scout makes an appearance in his homage to
Bruegel's Hunters in the Snow (Winter).

MYCHAEL BARRATT

Mychael has printed many dogs, either in the company of great artists or against a backdrop of great art. We show just a few images from his *Artists' Cats & Dogs* series. "The success of the Jackson Pollock piece [top left] comes from imagining the moment when Pollock realises his error [in painting the dog itself]." The print below left combines one of David Hockney's 'Big Splash' paintings with one of his portraits of his Dachshunds, Stanley and Boodgie. The image above is a homage to another of Mychael's favourite paintings, this time Edward Hopper's iconic 'Nighthawks'.

The fascinating print on page 11 results from a visit to see a retrospective of Pieter Bruegel the Elder. "I was so inspired that I started doing drawings for what would become 'Richmond Park' directly after leaving the gallery. The plate-making was fraught with setbacks. On the finished piece, traces of the errors remain, but have become some of the most successful elements, in that glorious way the etching gods have of rewarding shambolic artists. I include my own Dachshund, Scout, wherever possible and, as it was set in Richmond Park, I couldn't resist a reference to the infamous 'Fenton' incident.

"I was standing in front of the Michelin building in South Kensington when someone walked past with a French Bulldog. The idea came to me at that moment for a series of prints that combined my loves of Art Deco architecture and the films of Wes Anderson. I decided to do them as silkscreens with the intention that their symmetry and colour-drenched nostalgic feel would make them seem like stills from one of Anderson's films." The Michelin building appears opposite, and the Hoover building is featured on the back cover. *www.mychaelbarratt.com*

Wes Anderson's Dog – Michelin building (silkscreen). Far left, top: Jackson Pollock's Dog (aquatint). Far left, bottom: Hockney's Dog (etching & aquatint).
Left: Edward Hopper's Dog (etching & aquatint).

JACKIE CURTIS

Left: Marsh (linocut reduction print). Above: Marsh (monoprint).

Somerset-based Jackie Curtis is an artist and printmaker inspired by the natural world. She can often be found walking with her dog on the Somerset Levels observing the landscape and birds, sketch book and camera in hand; looking for materials and ideas to use in her varied methods of printmaking.

"We adopted a terrier called Marsh who was just full of character with the most amazing eyebrows and ability to 'chunter'. Although he was only with us a few years, this mischievous little dog couldn't fail to make an impression. He would greet you with his yappy bark and a non-stop wagging tail, but if you dropped something on the floor he would grab it before you could blink and would only drop it in exchange for a delicious treat.

"I produced two prints of Marsh, and the first [above right] is a monotype. His scruffy look lent itself to this technique which uses rags, cotton buds and cocktail sticks to draw into the ink. The second print [above left] is a linocut reduction print. Again, the detail of his wiry hair and the colours in his coat were ideal for this type of print."

Jackie works from her Somerset studio using relief techniques. Her monoprints are spontaneous, lively and innovative, often created as an immediate response to recent experiences. The collagraphs, produced from a collage of materials, are rich in texture and depth of tone. Linocuts are more intricate and stylised, with strong elements of pattern; while her woodblocks are influenced by natural grain, shape and flaws in the wood.

'This mischievous little dog couldn't fail to make an impression'

www.jcurtisart.com

HILARY PAYNTER

Wood engraver Hilary Paynter had at one point considered producing her own book of dog prints, with the artists commenting on the subject and/or the image. Instead, her work appears here – and Hilary has been a regular contributor of exceptional engravings to our various titles. Her 'Cat Show' and 'Cat Show II' prints were high points of *The Printmaker's Cat*, and we are delighted to feature 'Dogs' (above) and 'Dog Show' (on page 8) in this book.

Hilary has played a prominent role in the resurgence of wood engraving, both as an artist/engraver and through her work as Honorary Secretary and, later, Chairman of the reformed Society of Wood Engravers (SWE). She is a past president of the Royal Society of Painter-Printmakers (RE), and a Fellow of the Royal Society of Arts.

The engraving of the sleeping dog, Bosun (overleaf), is accompanied by sketches and the block used to create this popular edition

www.hilarypaynter.com

Page 15, left: Dogs. Page 15, top to bottom right: Bonnie; Gemma; Florrie. This page, clockwise from top left: Bosun; Bosun block and sketch; Chelsea; Moving the Dog (all wood engravings by Hilary Paynter — another, The Missing Glove, appears on the back cover).

HOWARD TOWLL

S hetland-based printmaker Howard tells us that "Scratch was a magnificent Border Collie/Whippet cross, which resulted in a very elegant, excitable and exceptionally agile dog. He could run like the wind, perform outrageous leaps and was as friendly, full of fun and as characterful as they come.

"Fortunately for Scratch, my job and spare-time interests involve a lot of walking the hills and shores of Shetland, so he never wanted for exercise (on which he thrived) and was always such great company. Unfortunately, when he was about four years old we discovered he had a heart condition, although his exceptional fitness and veterinary medicine meant that it never really affected his fast and ecstatic approach to life. The condition, however, was always going to cut his life short, and finally it caught up with him a few weeks shy of his 10th birthday. Although it was terribly sad at the time, Scratch had a fabulous life, full of freedom and fun, and was a dog's life well lived.

"Two of the prints here were done during his first few years when we used to walk down to the Bod of Nesbister and old fishing store at the end of the beach, where I would sit and sketch and Scratch would entertain himself chasing rabbits and crows. The third print, 'So Long Old Friend' [overleaf], is based on a drawing done during his final few weeks when his condition deteriorated. Unable to run down to the shore, he would stand on the garden wall above the woodpile, checking out the voe and surrounding hills, enjoying the summer sun, and barking his head off at passing cyclists and the postie emptying the mail box.

"Earlier in his life, in 'Rabbit Wrong-foots Dog' [right], Scratch – yelping with excitement and approaching at top speed – scatters the rabbits feeding on the links above the beach; he singles out one and chases it on to the beach. He is nearly level when the rabbit makes a sudden turn and Scratch skids and struggles to maintain his balance. In 'The Dog, the Crow and the Cursing Creeler' [overleaf], Scratch chases a crow feeding on something dead on the beach; meanwhile, a creeler goes by, reliving some argument or other, yelling profanities at the top of his voice as he pulls up the creels while I sit and sketch the scene."

www.howardtowll.com

Right: Rabbit Wrong-foots Dog. Page 18 left to right: So Long Old Friend; The Dog, the Crow and the Cursing Creeler (all woodcuts).

GUY ALLEN

Norfolk is Guy Allen's home, where he finds inspiration. "Growing up here, I have an affinity with and fascination for animals, for their quirks, strengths and fragility. The dog as a subject matter continues to be an inspiration in my work.

"I created these pieces by marrying the traditional technique of etching with a timeless subject matter and printmaking processes for a more contemporary twist. The stages involved in creating these original prints include etching, aquatint, screenprint and lithography.

"I use a stippling effect on the plate, a labour-intensive pointillist technique that gives the images a soft and evocative finish – perfect for fur, feathers and feelers. I use gold leaf, itself a delicate medium, to highlight the natural beauty, iridescence and fragility of the insect and animal world."

Guy graduated from Central Saint Martins School of Art in 2011, but discovered his passion for the traditional etching process while studying at the École Nationale

Supérieure Des Beaux-Arts in Paris in 2010. In 2012 he trained as an assistant printmaker at the highly respected Curwen Studios, Cambridge, under Mary Dalton and Stanley Jones, where he mastered other types of printmaking.

Today Guy works as a full-time artist, splitting his week between his London and Norfolk studios, accompanied by his trusty Wire-haired Dachshund, Loaf. The dog particularly inspires Guy – he delights in the technical skill required to capture dogs' musculature and movement.

Guy's work was exhibited in the Royal Academy's Summer Exhibition in 2013 and 2014, and was shortlisted in 2016. He has exhibited internationally in Dubai and New York, as well as having his etchings available on his home patch of Norfolk at the Red Dot Gallery in Holt. His work is housed in private collections in Los Angeles, San Francisco, New York, Singapore and Hong Kong. Guy has been featured in *House and Garden* and *Country Life* magazines.

www.guyallenart.com

Page 19: Norfolk Terrier and a Bumblebee. Facing page: Norfolk Terrier with Damselfly. Left: French Gold. Below left: Spaniel and Bumblebee (also on front cover). Below: Libby (all etchings).

JANE CONSTABLE

Jane has enjoyed making artwork since she could pick up a pencil. "I love printmaking, particularly the linocut technique. The most exciting stage of the process for me is the 'reveal' – as the result is so different each time. I have a passion for all things art and design, and this led me to create Inky Dog Studio – the perfect combination of art and printing ink, with a liberal amount of dog imagery thrown in!"

'Black Labrador in Grass' (far right, top) is a print inspired by a commissioned work made at the beginning of 2018. "Labradors are one of my favourite breeds, and I wanted to capture the serenity of the animal as he rested in the long grass on a summer's day."

'Dachshund' (far right, bottom) was made with a friend of Jane's in mind, who is crazy about the breed. "I particularly like the expression on the dog's face; if the print were

animated, she would be wagging her tail!"

'Delilah' (below) is a black Schnauzer whose owner commissioned a linocut print of her in this pose. The printed image was used as a logo/branding for a new dog grooming and therapy business start-up. "Delilah's owner was thrilled, and I am proud to have seen the wonderful shop sign featuring the image of my print."

'Blue Dog' on the far left is a limited-

edition 5-colour reduction linocut print. "I made this as a response to the theme of 'Reflection' when I was one of 20 printmakers selected to participate in an International Print Exchange in October 2018. My inspiration came from walks along Frinton beach in Essex, observing dogs and their owners enjoying the seaside out of season when animals are permitted on the beach."

'Kaiser' (overleaf) is a commissioned linocut print made in May 2019. "Kaiser is a black Labrador, and the print was commissioned as a birthday gift for his owner." Also shown is the block carved out and ready for a test print. "This was one of the most challenging blocks I have carved to date – mainly due to the small scale (the whole dog image inside an A5 area), capturing the expression in the eyes, and the smooth, glossy texture of Kaiser's fur."

'Trixie' (page 24) was a one-off commissioned linocut print made in 2018 – a black Cockapoo where the print was commissioned by a friend of her owners as a surprise gift. 'English Bulldog with Pizza' was inspired by a commissioned linocut in 2018. "The dog gives the appearance of standing guard over a slice of pizza – but, actually, the tasty slice is just a soft toy in her bed!"

www.inkydogstudio.com

Far left: Blue Dog (5-colour reduction linocut). Left: Delilah (single-block linocut). Top right: carved Delilah block. Bottom right: 2nd colour layer printed for Blue Dog. Far right, top: Black Labrador in Grass (single-block linocut). Far right, bottom: Dachshund (single-block linocut). Page 24 – top left: English Bulldog with Pizza (single-block linocut); bottom left: Trixie (single-block linocut); right: Kaiser (single-block linocut). Page 25: Kaiser block carved out and ready for a test print.

FIONA THOMSON

Fiona's drypoint etchings are worked by using a tool with a tiny industrial diamond tip to scratch directly into a soft metal such as zinc or copper. "I make a pencil drawing first, in these cases of my own dogs, then etch the drawing into the metal plate creating a groove with a raised 'burr' edge. This burr creates the soft and velvety look of a drypoint etching that distinguishes it from other printing methods.

"Once drawn the plate is carefully inked and wiped with muslin, leaving a degree of background ink (if required) and the etched channel loaded with ink. Damp printmaking paper is laid over the plate and then run through an etching press before being stacked between tissue paper and boards to dry flat. Drypoint is a fragile plate, and editions are usually limited by the quality because the press flattens the burr with each passing.

"In these prints I mainly feature Zoomie, my first Italian Greyhound who became quite famous via the internet and social media. He had quite a following and fan club for his stories and photographs, and people often asked for 'selfies' with him when he was out in public. In his lifetime I made hundreds of drawings, prints and paintings of him, and he featured on a popular range of greetings cards, Christmas cards and mugs. Sadly, Zoomie passed away in 2015, but his legacy remains in the artwork.

"'Waiting for Me' is about him in dog heaven waiting for us to be reunited. The print 'Waiting for You' is for my husband and his beloved Labrador, Milly."

Fiona, who lives in rural Scotland, is currently writing and illustrating a book about Zoomie – as well as another about a cousin of his, an Italian Greyhound called Peedie. Her main focus of work is dogs, particularly sighthounds such as Whippets and Italian Greyhounds.

www.fionathomson.com

Below from left to right: Zoomie 1; Waiting for Me; Waiting for You; Biscuit Please! Top, left to right: Pounce; Jump; Shaft of Sunlight (all drypoint etchings).

SARAH CEMMICK

A particularly stylish poodle by Sarah graces the flap of this book's front cover, representing one of her many dog-themed art cards based on original linocuts. There are many more pooches in the Cumbrian artist's range, several of which are featured here.

Living in the shadow of Crossfell in the beautiful Eden Valley, Sarah is inspired by the hares, songbirds and other creatures she sees in and around the surrounding fells. She studied environmental illustration at Sunderland University, which started a love affair with lino printing. Shortly afterwards, in 1998, she was awarded the Lloyds private banking award at the Society of Wildlife Artists' annual exhibition for her print 'Rhino Lino'. Since then her works have been exhibited throughout the UK and are held in private collections worldwide.

Her linocuts can be single-block, multi-block, jigsaw block or hand-coloured (a selection of Sarah's lino blocks can be seen on the right). At the time of writing, Sarah was working on new prints inspired by her latest muse, Bonzo the long-haired silver dapple Dachshund.

https://scemmick.wixsite.com/sarahcemmick

Facing page, clockwise from top left: Dotty Dog (jigsaw block linocut); Double Trouble (hand-coloured linocut); Teckel; Pug (both 2-block linocuts in gold and black). Above: Ready, steady... (single block linocut, hand-coloured with watercolour). Right: Frenchie (single-block linocut). Page 30, clockwise from top left: The Long and the Short of it 1 (2-block linocut in gold and black); The White Cavalier (single-block linocut); Spaniel (2-block linocut); The Long and the Short of it 2 (2-block linocut in gold and black).

All images on this page: Sarah Cemmick

KATHARINE GREEN

A self-confessed cat person, Katharine has never owned a dog herself. "My first encounter with dogs started when I was a very small child visiting my uncle and aunt in the Lake District. They loved Labradors, and Bucky was my great friend.

"Having spent most of my childhood drawing flora and fauna from the garden, I didn't attempt to paint dogs until my late teens when my policeman uncle Alan gave me my first commission to paint his Red Setter/Retriever cross Woody – rescued after he was abandoned and ended up at the police station.

"My love of printmaking was reignited only a few years ago in 2013 when I had one of my watercolours, 'Female Sparrow Hawk', exhibited at the Royal Academy's Summer Exhibition. I was so taken with all the wonderful prints on show that I immediately wanted to revisit the medium I first tried back at school – linocuts.

"I have now started exploring the art of reduction printing further. Several of the prints in this book use this method of relief printing. I start with the lightest colour and carve out each layer until all that is left is the darkest.

"Dogs now appear in a number of my prints. The charismatic Cavapoo Harvey [page 32] is a Cavalier King Charles Spaniel and Poodle cross who belongs to my cousin Ginny and her husband Adrian. I have heard from a number of people that they are very sweet natured, and this is so true of Harvey.

"'Good Boy' [below left] is a very handsome black Labrador called Dexter who lives next door to me. When he first moved in he was the dearest archetypal puppy. At around 12 weeks old he looked very smart in his red collar. I couldn't resist

producing a print of him sitting to attention in the garden.

"'Up to Mischief' [below] is based on my good friend's Cockapoo puppy, Fenn, who has livened up the household with his intelligent, mischievous personality. This print evolved after spending the morning in their garden. Making sure no one was watching, Fenn busily started trying to hide his Denta stick among the shrubs – but couldn't resist the flower pots! 'Downward Dog' [far right] is a bit of fun inspired by the playful Fenn posing with his ball – adopting his version of the yoga position 'downward-facing dog'.

"Deni [page 31] is a rather beautiful toffee blonde Cocker Spaniel who reminds me of Lady from Disney's *Lady and the Tramp*. I wanted to create a portrait of her to capture that gaze of love and trust that dogs have for their owners." www.katharinegreen.com

Left: Harvey (reduction linocut). Far right: Downward Dog (reduction linocut).

*Page 31, left to right: Good Boy (linocut hand-painted with watercolour); Deni (reduction linocut).
Below: Up to Mischief (a series of four linocuts).
Left: Mischief sketches.*

ANNA TOSNEY

Anna points out that Border Collies are a popular breed in the Yorkshire Dales as they make great sheep dogs. "I love watching them out at work with the farmers, helping to round up the sheep or sitting on the back of a Land Rover or quad. They are very intelligent dogs, and each has his/her own personality. You can see their minds at work and almost work out from their facial expressions what they are thinking.

"Having also had Border Collies as pets, I've had the opportunity to watch

them up close as well as from a distance. The dogs in my work are modelled on my dog Floss [below centre] and on a couple of Border Collies, Zak and Jesse, who 'help' run the Cherrydidi Gallery in Keswick, which sells my work.

"My main printmaking technique is drypoint/monoprint. In my case, a sharp steel

Facing page, left: Off to Work (another colourway appears on page 10). Centre: Floss in the studio. Below: Who's the Guilty One (another colourway appears on page 6). Bottom: printing of 'Who's the Guilty One' (all images drypoint/monoprint).

tool is used to scratch directly into the surface plexiglass. I rub thick printmaking ink into the line, then wipe the surface clean. When put through a printing press, this gives a black, velvety line [plate and printed image, page 35 bottom right].

"In monoprint, which is often confused with monotype, a single underlying image is used, such as an etched plate or a screen print. In my case I use a drypoint plate. This is then made unique through the process of hand colouring or surface alteration to the printed image. A series of monoprints may be similar, but no two are ever the same."

www.annatosney.com

Left: Off We Go (drypoint/monoprint). Below: wiping the inked plate.

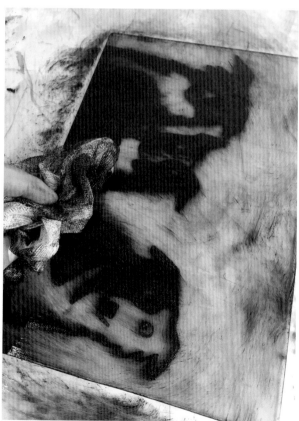

CHRIS DAUNT

Chris Daunt is a provider of traditional endgrain wood engraving blocks used by many successful printmakers. A former Cistercian monk in the Scottish Borders, he is nowadays based in the heart of Thomas Bewick country, where he produces beautiful wood engravings and teaches the art. He is currently Chairman of the Society of Wood Engravers (SWE) and contributed some striking images to our book *The Printmaker's Cat*, so it is good to see that he can also turn his hand to dogs.

Born in Bedlington, Chris studied Fine Art at Newcastle Polytechnic, later obtaining an Honours Degree in English Literature at the University of Newcastle.

He indulges in the relatively uncommon practice of multi-block colour wood engraving to great effect, as shown by 'Woody' and 'White Dog in Winter' below.

www.chrisdaunt.com

Clockwise from top left: Woody; Miko; White Dog in Winter; Gill the Collie (all wood engravings).

ANDREW STOCK

Wildlife artist Andrew Stock is well travelled, sketching and painting in Africa, Antarctica and even the Himalayas. However, the etching and aquatint shown here finds him much closer to home, as it features his Lurcher, Bandit, in very comfortable pose.

"Bandit was a terrific dog; he looked quite intimidating but was the gentlest of Lurchers. He was full of energy and would accompany me on my long, marathon training runs as well as always stealing the best seat in the house, usually the sofa."

Andrew has been painting full time since leaving Sherborne School in 1978. For more than 25 years, etching (on copper plate in the traditional way) has also formed an important part of his creative repertoire. This etching measures 20 x 25cm and is tricky to print with two colours inked carefully on to the one plate.

Andrew's subject matter is primarily wildlife, especially birds, and he also paints still lifes and landscapes. He has been a Fellow of the Royal Society of Painter-Printmakers (RE) since 2005, and a member of the Society of Wildlife Artists (S WL A) since 1983. Initially serving as Secretary of the S WL A he went on to become President from 2004 to 2009. He has also served as a Governor at the Federation of British Artists. Andrew is now an Honorary Vice President of the S WL A, and continues to exhibit etchings, watercolours and oils at its annual exhibition.

www.andrewstock.co.uk

Bandit (etching and aquatint)

SUE CLEMENTS

Sue has been attending the printmaking classes of Amanda Averillo in Sissinghurst, whose own work appears on page 115 of this collection. Sue's print below, 'Alf in Daisies', is a monoprint where inks rolled on to acetate are 'wiped off' in such a way as to create the image ready for the press.

"This was inspired by a photo taken on the last camping trip with him, enjoying the breeze and smells in the field of tall daisies. The print is currently hanging on my daughter's bedroom wall.

"My interests are drawing and printmaking, enjoying texture and shadow. My love of dogs, along with the buildings, flora and gentle landscape in Kent, inspire my work."

email: sueclements84@gmail.com

Alf in Daisies
(monoprint)

HELEN FAY

At the time of submission for this book, Helen's print 'Whippet' (below) was on show at the Royal Academy Summer Exhibition. As with the other images shown here, the printmaking technique is etching, using copper plate.

"Copper is a lovely material for fine, subtle mark-making. I attempt to make my images sparse and balanced between the subject and the space in which they sit or stand. The focus is on the character and stance of the dog I am drawing.

"Shakespeare [page 42] is one of my most memorable dogs. I drew him as a puppy where his giant lion paws gave some indication of the huge boy he was going to grow into; and as an adolescent flopped on a chair, exhausted after a long walk. He's the biggest, softest family dog imaginable – and his best friend is Wilf the cat.

"For many years my work has been about the beauty, dignity and character of animals. The poise and movement of animals, their behaviour and nature is an area I find endlessly fascinating. I like to think of them observing the world as I am observing them.

"At the moment I am focusing on how animals are intertwined with our domestic and family life. I want to capture moments such as a dog flopped on a chair after a long walk or watching the world while their owner stops for a coffee. I hope to capture these small moments that surround us when we have animals in our life.

"My influences include Japanese and Chinese prints and drawings and the 19th- and 20th-century European artists who were influenced by them. I love the landscape paintings of Mondrian and Schiele, and the work of Bonnard. I have long been interested in the work of 20th-century war artists such as Nash and Ravilious: the clarity of their work is hugely impressive. Lastly, I would mention two great influences in natural history illustration, Thomas Bewick and Charles Tunnicliffe. Both these men, in their work and curiosity about the natural world, have been a lifelong inspiration."

www.helenfay.co.uk

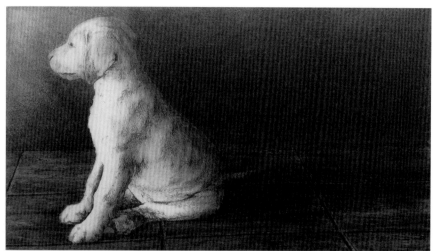

Page 40: Whippet. Page 41: Arthur. Left, top to bottom: Shakespeare; Pippin; Floss. Below and bottom: Hamish; After the Walk (all copperplate etchings by Helen Fay).

'I drew Shakespeare as a puppy where his giant lion paws gave some indication of the huge boy he was going to grow into… He's the biggest, softest family dog imaginable – and his best friend is Wilf the cat'

MARIAN CARTER

Tess the Dachshund belongs to Marian's neighbour and good friend Michaela. The print is a polymer etching, and it was produced for an exhibition inspired by Roald Dahl's short stories entitled 'A Twist on Dahl'.

"In a story called 'The Landlady', a sweet little Dachshund sleeps in front of a fire. As is often the case with Roald Dahl tales, there is more to this than meets the eye.

"Tess is a lovely affectionate and friendly little dog. I drew her in my sketchbook then painted and drew her on to true-grain film and used this to make a printing plate.

"The film is placed on a metal plate coated in light-sensitive polymer and exposed to ultraviolet light. The plate is then washed with water and becomes an etched plate that can be inked up and put through a press like a traditional etching."

Marian lives in a Buckinghamshire village, and recurring themes in her work are animals and birds.

www.mariancarterart.co.uk

A Cosy Bed (polymer etching)

ALISON READ

A book featuring dogs and printmaking wouldn't be complete without Alison's amusing canine creations – but the sheer volume means making a selection is a challenge.

"I love all animals, but I really love dogs. You always know exactly where you are with a dog and, in return, they accept us without question with all our flaws. It is a perfect relationship, a true unconditional love.

"My current best friend is a black Labrador called Bear. I sometimes think that he doesn't know he is a dog. I probably credit him with more intelligence than he actually has, but that's because to my eyes he is just perfect!

"Obviously he is my printmaking muse, and there are clearly a lot of dog lovers out there who feel the same way. My most popular prints are those with Bear taking centre stage."

Alison chose printmaking as her medium as soon as she was allowed in the print room during her time at Newcastle University, where she studied for her first degree in Fine Art.

She then ran the Printmaking Workshop at Lincoln University for nine years, completing her MA, learning a lot about practical printmaking, and exhibiting her own work. This led to her going it alone as a commercial artist-printmaker – specialising in hand-made original prints in a variety of methods including screenprints, etchings, woodcuts, linocuts and aquatinting.

The subject matter is quirky, fun and mainly animal humour, but always different. Alison's upbringing on a farm explains her preoccupation with animals in her work as she literally spent most of her waking hours surrounded by them – cows, cats, dogs and chickens were her constant companions.

"Years ago I read Milan Kundera's *The Unbearable Lightness of Being* and it made me weep for days, not only because it is beautifully written, but because of the dog, Karenin. It sums up for me the part that the unconditional love of a dog plays in our lives. Whatever happens along the way, our relationship with our dog stays exactly the same."

email: alisonread1@googlemail.com

Above: Posh Paws (etching). Top right: Indecent Proposal (linocut). Below, left to right: Sausage Sandwich (linocut); Brigitte Bardog (etching); Puggy Dog Eyes (linocut); Phileas Dogg (screenprint); It Wasn't Me (etching).

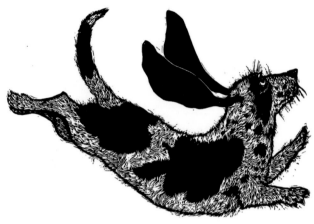

Above, left to right: Pug Rug (etching); Flying Without Wings (linocut); Is it Ready Yet? (linocut); Bella (etching). Below, left to right: Behind Closed Doors; All Cakes Come With a Side-order of Staring Labrador; Sir Dog Weimer (all linocuts). The Best Friend (etching) appears on page 3 and the linocut Bone is reproduced on page 5.

NINA SAGE

Chester, Nina's Standard Poodle, takes a keen interest in all aspects of his mistress's printmaking, as evidenced by the picture in the middle. "He usually sits on whatever I am trying to sketch. He 'helps' me cut the lino by resting his head on my arm, and closely supervises my editioning. In short, he can be relied on to get in the way!

"Chester proved a challenge to capture in a print because he's so black it was hard to get the definition and movement of his coat without lightening him too much." Nina explains that the print on the far right works as there was strong light on one side of him – "but I still had to be careful with the balance of tones so that you can see his curls while keeping him black. My family laughed as this lino shows Chester in a typical pose leaning against a chair with his paws precisely crossed. His wistful expression was the result of my husband, whom he adores, having the temerity to go out without him.

"When I begin a new print I start by pulling together reference material: sketches

From left to right: carved vinyl block; Chester keeping an eye on the prints; Wistful (reduction linocut on vinyl).

from life, photographs and notes, etc, and make a few scruffy thumbnails. I sketch my composition on to tracing paper, cut to the same size as my block so the design is easily reversed on to it. I also scan and print the reversed design, and colour this with coloured pencils. I work from this reversed coloured drawing though I don't follow it religiously. I may add colours with different small rollers when I am printing, creating variable editions.

"My favourite printmaking method is linocut, both reduction and multi-block. I say lino but I don't actually like lino at all, preferring to use vinyl floor tiles instead. They take a fine line without crumbling in my press, and when I want to change my Caligo safewash ink colours I can just rinse the tile under the tap without it warping. As I like detail and use lots of colours in each layer, vinyl is perfect for the way I work."

www.ninasage.co.uk

JANIS GOODMAN

Leeds-based printmaker Janis Goodman works out of her own studios, "which have pretty much taken over the house. I melt my wax grounds on top of the cooker, and soak my paper in the bath!

"I learnt etching through an evening class at Leeds School of Art, and was immediately very attracted to this form of printmaking. I love the mixture of technical problems and happenstance that influence the final image. I was lucky to find that I made the sort of prints that other people wanted to buy. In this way, printmaking gradually became my sole occupation.

"I make etchings that focus on the relationships between the natural and urban worlds. Every work is individually inked and hand printed using a heavy iron etching press. My prints are preoccupied with the patterns formed by roofs, windows and chimneys and how they contrast with the organic forms of plants and birds. I love pattern but I also find great interest in the ways in which the repetition is interrupted. My pictures are small narratives in which different elements meet and interact."

Janis is one of a number of artists in this collection who has made previous appearances in our books, with her prints reproduced in *The Illustrated Garden* and in *The Little Chicken Book*.

www.janisgoodman.co.uk

Below: Gooseherd. Right: Molly.
Far right: Dog Days (all etchings).

RUTH GREEN

Ruth has recently relocated from Birmingham to the Welsh Borders, where she will continue to produce amusing and colourful silkscreen prints by hand, with dogs forming a significant part of her portfolio. She is currently planning and building a new print studio near Oswestry.

Her work is inspired by mid-century design and pattern and by the British countryside. In 2011, Tate Publishing produced Ruth's first illustrated book for children, *Noisy Neighbours*, which has been followed by *Stanley's Plan* (2014) and *Hedgehog Holidays* (2017).

Her work has appeared in *Elle Decoration*, and she exhibits regularly throughout the UK.

"Dogs feature a lot as my subject matter. I love dogs and wouldn't be without them. Currently we have a Saluki named Bert (who features in 'Butter Wouldn't Melt'), and Gorgeous George, our brindle Greyhound. My working day seems to hang around their routine, and I have always found dog walks to be the perfect time to plan ideas for new prints." Another of Ruth's screenprints, 'Stanley', appears on page 9.

"I've been experimenting with some more painterly ways to screenprint

recently, and the 'Butter Wouldn't Melt' print demonstrates a screen/monoprint technique that uses stencils to make multiples. This style gives more texture in the way of brush marks and a variation between each print."

www.ruthgreendesign.com

Facing page, from top left: We Live Here; Bailey; Longshanks. Above, clockwise from top left: To the Park; Lucy; Butter Wouldn't Melt; Buttercups; Gorgeous George (all screenprints).

ANDY ENGLISH

Living and working just outside Ely in Cambridgeshire, Andy is a versatile and talented wood engraver capable of turning his hand to almost any subject – hence his appearance in virtually all of our multi-artist printmaking books.

"Of all the creatures I have made engravings of, it seems to me that my images of dogs are always portraits. There is always a definite personality to be captured and the setting is always important. Some of my wood engravings have cats passing through or lingering in a warm spot. However, the dogs are more likely to occupy or even seem to own their place.

"Sparky [below left] is a good example. He is a Border Terrier who appreciates this comfy chair, which even has a Border Terrier cushion. I only met him late in his life when he had lost much of his spark, but he gave the impression of being a convivial companion and seldom shifted from this comfy spot.

"The Springer Spaniel dominates the landscape I have pictured him in. This was a commission that had to convey more than the dog; but the image is, nevertheless, much more of a canine portrait than anything else.

"The Old English Sheepdog [below right] is called Nana and was an important component of a bookplate commission. I worked from a photograph of a suitably windswept Nana, and it was great fun to show the movement of the hair with long, sinuous lines engraved with my 'spitsticker'. This is the burin I use the most, and it is perfect for cutting the curved lines and

carrying out the equivalent of drawing on the endgrain woodblock.

"'Waiting for the Boys' [below, far right, with sketch above it] is a more personal engraving. It features Bella, our Lurcher, who is no longer around to steal food and bark at the doorbell. She was most likely a cross between a Greyhound and a German Shepherd, and was a fast, elegant dog with very expressive eyebrows. She could also be loud and naughty (she was a rescue dog).

"This engraving shows Bella looking out the window, waiting for the school bus to bring the boys home. She would sit still like a statue of the Egyptian god Anubis. With her keen hearing, she would be the first to greet the bus coming along the road." *www.andyenglish.com*

'She would sit still like a statue of the Egyptian god Anubis. With her keen hearing, she would be the first to greet the bus coming along the road'

From left to right: Sparky; Springer Spaniel; Old English Sheepdog; Waiting for the Boys (all wood engravings).

SANCHIA LEWIS

London-based artist Sanchia made a striking contribution to *The Printmaker's Cat* with her bold and colourful etchings. Here we are able to reproduce her entire dog portfolio, with both images based on intaglio and relief etchings printed from a zinc plate with areas of "deep biting and hard-ground detail".

For 'Firehouse Dog' [below], Sanchia explains that she was inspired by a 19th-century hooked rug seen in the American Museum near Bath. "Dalmatians were used in America to run alongside fire carriages; they could keep pace with the horses and protect them from animals and other dogs,

even over long distances. When a fire alarm sounded, the Dalmatians would run out of the firehouse, barking to let people know that they should get out of the way; once the wagon was out on the street, the dogs would run beside it.

"Horses are afraid of fire, and the

Dalmatians' presence could distract and comfort the horses as they pulled the wagon closer to a blaze. The Dalmatians also stood guard near the wagon to make sure that no one stole the firefighter's belongings, equipment or horses. The tradition of Dalmatians accompanying carriages was probably started by 18th-century aristocrats. Dalmatians are still used in the USA as firehouse mascots."

Sanchia studied printmaking at the City & Guilds of London Art School. On leaving college, she trained as an editioner with the etcher Paul Bisson, before receiving an award from The Prince's Trust that enabled her to set up her London studio.

www.sanchialewis.co.uk

Left: Firehouse Dog. Below: Dappled Dog (both zinc-plate etchings).

EMILY SMITH POLYBLANK

Top left: Come Play With Me. Bottom left: Warm Spring Morning. Right, top to bottom: Two Hounds; Run; Long Dog (all woodcuts).

The inspiration for Emily's work comes from her surroundings. "My mother owns a smallholding with lots of animals in the countryside around the North Downs of Kent, where I grew up. Due to both my parents being artists, I was encouraged at an early age to sketch from life."

As well as nowadays being part of a farm cooperative, with four people running a smallholding in Kent, Emily works in her father's old studio. Royal Academy-trained, he was an excellent portrait and landscape painter until his early death in 1988. "My mother, a talented painter in her own right, has also influenced and encouraged me."

Emily studied at Maidstone College of Art and Farnham College of Art. Her main printmaking media are woodcut and lino. "Wood grain has a lovely natural texture of its own that can control the images and also adds to them. I love to put dogs in my prints to show their lovely forms, and I hope their flow of movement is captured and expressed in a medium that can sometimes be a bit rigid."

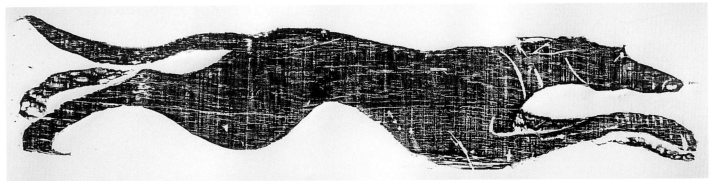

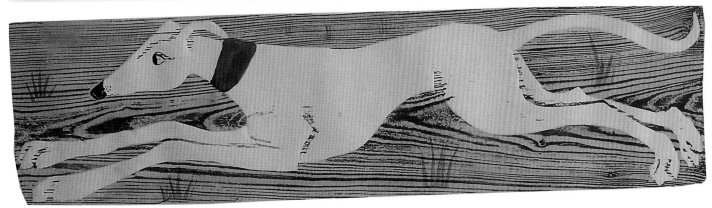

Her woodcuts and linoprints have now been selected on seven occasions for the Royal Academy Summer Exhibitions, with the latest being the 2019 show that includes her biggest woodcut print to date.

www.emilysmithpolyblank.co.uk

Opposite page, from top to bottom: United; Many Dogs; Bedlington Whippet Meets Irish Wolfhounds; Go On Dogs, Run Away. Below and right: Running Rings; Sit (all woodcuts).

ROSALIND FORSTER

Mr Bailey is the dog in the print on the left, and lives in Tasmania. The artist, Rosalind Forster, splits her time between Greece and the UK. All in all, a relatively exotic combination.

"This dog is the adored companion of Richard King, with whom I used to exhibit in Sydney in the 1980s. He then retired to Tasmania. The reduction linocut is printed in 10 colours on Japanese paper in a small edition of 10."

Rosalind trained initially as a graphic designer, and worked for several years for a London design group. She subsequently moved to Derbyshire where she set up her own print workshop to produce posters (now collectors' items) for the Derby Playhouse and Winster Wakes.

With the acquisition of a full-sized Albion press, she developed her technique of lino cutting using the reduction process.

www.rosalindforster.moonfruit.com

HANNAH FIRMIN

The unusual dog-themed linocut print on the right has an equally unusual story behind it. Produced by Hannah Firmin, who made a wonderful contribution to our book *The Illustrated Garden*, the original illustration was created for the *Sunday Times* many years ago.

"It was made to illustrate an article about a farmer in Australia who had a glut of lemons that started to ferment and gave him the idea to turn them into alcoholic lemonade – a new idea that was popular for a while. His brand was to be called 'Two Dogs'. This was all I was told, so I made the illustration with dogs I liked. The label image actually featured two Bulldogs, I think, but I wasn't told this!

"Whatever happened to the drink? Anyway, I have sold a few of these prints over the years, although it is not an edition as each one is coloured differently."

www.hannahfirmin.com

GERI WADDINGTON

A member and past chair of the Society of Wood Engravers (SWE), Geri Waddington engraves on traditional endgrain woodblocks, and sometimes on resin blocks, producing limited editions on a Victorian hand press. She also creates book illustrations, and has contributed to a number of our earlier titles, including *The Printmaker's Cat*, *The Elegant Fowl*, *The Little Chicken Book* and *The Illustrated Garden*.

As well as being a member of the SWE, Geri is a 'brother' of the Art Workers' Guild, and one of the founders of the International Academic Printmaking Alliance. She exhibits extensively across the UK, and as far east and west as China and the USA. Her work is in public and private collections, including the Ashmolean Museum, Bristol Museum and Art Gallery, the Hunt Institute for Botanical Documentation in Pittsburgh, and the Central Academy of Fine Arts in Beijing. She trained at The Slade School of Fine Art.

Dogs feature in several of her engravings. 'Diggory' (facing page, bottom) was found wandering the

streets of Stevenage, hence his name (from the French for 'lost one'). "The gentlest dog in the world, we were obliged to have him neutered by the rescue kennels, but our vet declined on the grounds that 'he needed all the testosterone he could muster'. A darling, much missed..."

'Dog Star' (opposite, right), meanwhile, features Geri's third Border Collie rescue, "the very handsome Shep". Inspired by the well-known(sic) Christmas carol 'While Sheepdogs Watched', this engraving's trade secret is that the pose was achieved not by star-gazing but by Geri's husband holding a biscuit above Shep's nose!

"'Daisy' [opposite, far left] features the totally daft Lurcher rescued by my brother and enjoying a restful retirement; while 'Harry Christmas' [above right] immortalises the Cocker Spaniel puppy who arrived a few weeks before Christmas two years ago and has stolen our hearts. Yes, he did also steal shoes, socks and the post if we were not quick enough, but those big brown eyes and boundless enthusiasm make it impossible to take offence. And, despite this engraving, he hasn't actually found a nice juicy piece of boxwood to chew – yet!"

www.geriwaddington.com

'The gentlest dog in the world, we were obliged to have him neutered by the rescue kennels, but our vet declined on the grounds that he needed all the testosterone he could muster'

Far left: Daisy. Left: Dog Star. Top right: Harry Christmas. Right: Diggory (all wood engravings).

CARL BORGES

Freddie is Carl's Lakeland Terrier, and he is the star of all but one picture here. "'Freddie with Ball' [facing page] is an idealised version of our garden in Combs, Suffolk. He loves playing football and is very good at it – if he could only learn the rules!

"'Afternoon Doze' [left] is of my wife Sue with Freddie asleep on her lap in an armchair in our dining room. When he is very relaxed he lies on his back to have his chest tickled."

We have reproduced a detail below from Carl's print 'Breakfast at Landguard Point, Felixstowe', as it shows rather more of Freddie and less of the giant container ship and cranes at the port. The whole print is shown on page 68.

"This is the three of us having breakfast at the cafe which, coupled with a walk to Felixstowe Pier, is a favourite day out.

"These are all multi-block linocuts. Two of them use four colours, but 'Freddie with Ball' uses five. ▶

Left: Afternoon Doze. Below: detail from Breakfast at Landguard Point, Felixstowe. Right: Freddie With Ball (all multi-block linocuts).

"'Gwyn, Myrtle and Lupin' [below left] are our neighbours' (Harriet, Joe and Florence) German Pointers. Very lively but lovely dogs. Unfortunately Gwyn is no longer with us, but her place has been taken by Medlar. A very different but just as lovely dog with very long ears for a Pointer. This is a reduction print."

Carl has been a printmaker for around 15 years, and is largely self taught. Most of his images are relief prints and paintings, although he also uses other printmaking techniques. His work also features in the Mascot Media publications *Suffolk Jewels* and *The Illustrated Garden*. He enjoys exploring the patterns, shapes and textures found in nature.

"My work proceeds through a series of sketches and sometimes photographs," he explains. "The first sketches are usually from memory or imagination. As the composition develops, a combination of sketches from the scene and photographs are used to fill in any required details. The completed composition is then transferred on to the surface of the lino or wood block ready for the 'cutting away' process."

www.carlborges.co.uk

Top: Breakfast at Landguard Point, Felixstowe
(multi-block linocut).
Bottom: Gwyn, Myrtle and Lupin (reduction linocut) —
both by Carl Borges.

NEIL BOUSFIELD

Neil describes himself as a "contemporary engraver", and finds that a discipline that combines drawing, making and thinking "provides me with an evolving process to explore concepts and techniques".

"The physicality of the process, the tactile nature of inks, papers, blocks, craft skills and the haptic feedback gained through the very act of engraving is fundamental. However, the simple nature of the process provides no room for fuzziness as there is a clear and direct relationship between hand and mind."

Neil says that different prints allow innovation: "The use of new materials, multiple blocks, colour and the reduction process all seem to lie on the edge of the tradition of wood engraving."

On moving to the north-east Norfolk coast towards the end of 2011, Neil began

Right: Skinny Dog in a Green Chair.
Below: Waggy Dog (both wood engravings).

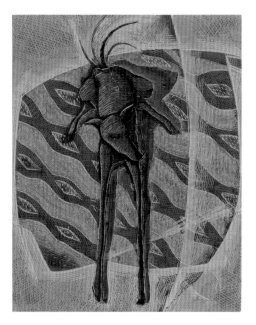

a series of drawings as a direct response to connect to his new home, with work commencing on the wood engravings in 2012. 'Big Boy' (page 72) was completed in 2013; 'Taking in the View' (page 72) and 'On Eccles Beach' (appearing as the background to these pages) in 2014; and 'Sea Side Games' (above) plus 'Taking the Sea Air' (opposite) in 2016.

For Neil, the smell of the sea "imparts a unique sensory experience of place", while works such as 'Sea Side Games' "explore the games we play to defend the land against the relentless encroachment of the sea".

"The work is concerned with the emotional construct of place. Primarily, two strands of narrative are interwoven within neural code in the hippocampus to activate place cells. This allows us to project values and experiences encapsulated within daily routine and experience, or dog walking and narrative of places held in history, archaeology and artefacts.

"Walking the dogs along a coast rich in stories, history and beach finds is a process that promotes place attachment. The Whippet is a dog like no other; beautiful, elegant, good to live with and wonderful to draw. I make work about place, and the way I experience places is through walking and drawing with Whippets."

www.neilbousfield.com

Background: On Eccles Beach. Left: Sea Side Games.
Above: Taking the Sea Air (all wood engravings).

'The Whippet is a dog like no
other; beautiful, elegant,
good to live with and wonderful
to draw. I make work about
place, and the way I experience
places is through walking
and drawing with Whippets'

Top: Big Boy.
Bottom: Taking In The View
(both wood engravings) — both
Neil Bousfield. Neil's wood
engraving Runners is reproduced
on page 6, while Me Whippets
appears on the front cover.

NANCY POWER

Featured here is a reduction linocut print of Nancy's dog Tilly. "We had this beautiful girl for over 15 years, but sadly had to say goodbye just before Christmas 2018. This print just personifies her..."

East Midlands-based Nancy is a self-taught printmaker who spent more than 25 years in the clothing design industry. "A timely redundancy gave me the impetus to pursue printmaking full time, and I have never looked back."

The main focus of her practice is creating reduction linocut prints. "I'm excited by the 'absolute' decision-making that this process requires. Many of my images are printed from dark to light, as I am intrigued as to how the colours perform quite differently and give some unexpected and surprising results."

Her work features the countryside and coastal scenes, plants, animals and still life. "I love nature and the contrasts of light throughout the seasons, which I try to portray in my work."

www.nancypowerprints.com

SUE FARROW-JONES

Below: Albemarle Summerhouse and Hounds.
Right: Moondancers v2 (both linocuts).

Sue Farrow-Jones originally studied textiles, but also spent many years at The Dartington Print Workshop. Now retired and living in South Devon, she produces linocuts, screen-printed lampshades and watercolours, many of which are inspired by her Wolfhound and Lurcher hounds.

"'Ludo and Magic in Albemarle Garden' [overleaf] is the view from the kitchen window

on the day Ludo arrived; 'Shhh... Wolfhound Asleep!' [above left and right] shows Magic settled for a snooze on a three-seater settee; 'Moondancers' [page 75] features Magic and Ludo playing with Deerhound friends Hattie and Millie; 'Albemarle Summerhouse and Hounds' [page 74] shows Harley, Zappa and Riff-raff in Albemarle garden with a carved wooden hare; and as for 'Magic and Ludo at Albemarle' [top left], we were lucky to get somewhere to sit down in the lounge – quick, an empty chair!"

runningdogprints.wordpress.com

Above, clockwise from top left: Magic and Ludo at Albemarle; Ludo and Magic in Albemarle Garden; Shhh Wolfhound Asleep! v2; Shhh Wolfhound Asleep! (all linocuts by Sue Farrow-Jones).

YSABEL WINZAR

S outh Devon-based painter-printmaker Ysabel's work reflects both rapid glimpses and concentrated observations from her varied "stuff of life" which, since childhood, has been involved with art. With every image, she aims to capture and translate that first moment which caught her attention.

'The Mighty Midget' (left) depicts the "very small" Border Terrier named Midget. "We have shared many happy hours throwing and retrieving sticks in the stream, and I always tire before she does. In 'Dog Days of Summer' [below], another Border Terrier, Grace, looks out wistfully to the garden, frustrated by the pane of glass separating her from the next adventure."

Both works are aluminium plate etchings made using non-toxic ground on the plate and etched with a copper sulphate mordant. They are printed using water-based inks on Hahnemuhle paper.

email: ysabelw@btinternet.com

Above: The Mighty Midget. Right: Dog Days of Summer (both etchings).

'We have shared many happy hours throwing and retrieving sticks in the stream, and I always tire before she does'

ROZ HOWLING

Roz has been experimenting with printmaking for the past 10 years, inspired by the work of Elizabeth Fink, Andy Warhol and Franz Marc, who all incorporated animals, her passion, in their work.

Dogs are one of Roz's favourite subjects to draw and print. "They are full of character and expression that is not only unique to each breed, but to each individual." Roz's first dog, Winnie, a black Labrador, is featured in multiple prints including the portrait below,

the monoprint on the left and in a linocut on page nine.

Roz's work is varied in both style and technique. Having started her printmaking career with linoprinting, she has since branched out, experimenting with collagraph, drypoint etching, aquatint, monoprinting and hybrid printing techniques.

"I'm attracted to printmaking because the process of pulling multiple prints from a single plate enables me to experiment with

colour, mark-making and texture," she says. "I enjoy comparing the outcomes of various prints pulled from the same plate, eliciting which elements I prefer, and using this to inspire later works and further print editions.

"I enjoy experimenting, and am always evolving my technique and style in response to the subject of my inspiration."

www.rozannaartist.co.uk

*Left: Labrador (linocut).
Right: Wellie (linocut).
Facing page, clockwise from
top left: Winnie (monoprint);
Elsie (linocut); Spaniel (linocut
with mono and pastel); Twiglet
(linocut). Roz Howling's linocut
Winnie Sitting appears on page 9.*

MAX ANGUS

Left: Just Five Minutes Earlier (linocut). Right: what's happening next? — Kessie in the shadow of the press.

Wildlife printmaker Max confesses that her best friend prior to Border Collie Kessie was of the feline persuasion.

"I had accidentally shared my home with a silver short-haired cat, who was with me for 12 years. He was quite a character and very dog-like. He was happy to go on a lead and travel in the car to see friends.

"A few months after he passed away I heard about a litter of Border Collie puppies born just a couple of miles away. They were all reserved with a waiting list. As much as I would have loved a dog, I knew that a dog craves attention far more than a cat. And I still thought that one day I would find another silver cat...

"When the pups were around seven weeks old, I received a call. Would I like to meet the tiny black and white bitch pup? For some unknown reason she had been declined by other potential buyers. A little woolly bundle was carried in to the breeder's front room. At that time the pup's eyes were still blue, later to become brown. She stared at each face as she tried to catch a gaze in return. That was enough; I had met my new best friend. A week later 'Kessie' came home.

"From six months old Kessie was my companion when out sketching – she would lie just in front of me. It could be due to the time spent watching the birds, but Kessie seemed to welcome them in the garden...

"That first winter she was too young to step out in the brief periods of snowfall. The following winter was very different. One late afternoon, just as the temperature started to fall, the snow came thick and fast. An hour later, the garden was covered in a carpet of white. Kessie looked in disbelief and amazement. Then, as boldly as a timid young Border Collie could, with a backward glance, she tested the white stuff with one paw. Fear over, she ran and ran for all she was worth.

"It snowed on and off for a few days. I managed to sketch bits of Kessie running. All the bits were then built into the sketches to create the plan for the 2-block linocut 'First Snow' [top left].

"The following year the blanket of snow fell again. Kessie stood there and looked. I grabbed my sketchbook. Again, she tested the snow with one paw. This time there was a little run of a few yards, hesitation, but then she returned. I had to go with her. With her head down, she inspected the snow and walked round the garden. The garden was now full of dog paw prints. It was as if she were walking up and down wondering where all the footprints had come from.

"Kessie likes routine. Monday to Friday is when she expects to be either taken for a walk or spend the day in the studio. Some days paperwork has to be done. At these times, Kessie takes up position by the patio window [see below]." This print, 'Just Waiting', narrowly failed to be shown at the Royal Academy Summer Exhibition.

On page 80, 'Just Five Minutes Earlier' captures Kessie on a cold day when she was prepared to tolerate the fire in the living room. "It is about those times when everything is quiet, but there's pending news or visitors on their way. Within five minutes everything can change."

www.maxangus.co.uk

Top left: First Snow (linocut), with preliminary sketch above. Bottom left: Walk With Me (linocut). Right: Just Waiting (linocut), with preliminary sketch above.

KAY McDONAGH

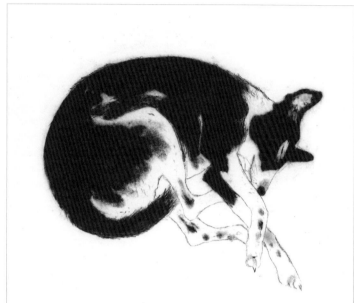

Sidmouth-based printmaker Kay McDonagh is perhaps best known for her etchings of dogs and cats, having contributed to two versions of our book *The Printmaker's Cat*. She has also provided prints for both versions of *The Artful Hare*, while the occasional rabbit, sheep or even rat have been known to sneak into her large animal-themed portfolio.

Recent years have seen her move away from traditional acid-etched copperplate etchings to drypoint: she etches directly on to an acrylic plate, before inking then hand-printing with a press built from scratch some 25 years ago in the East Midlands.

Kay strives to capture the character of her animal subjects in her prints, usually with an element of fun. The more these single images are studied, the more complex the patterns, shapes and faces seem to become.

email: kaymcdonagh@hotmail.com

Facing page, clockwise from top left: Shut Eye; Dream on Dreamer; What's Up; Rescued; Didn't Get Caught. Clockwise from top left: Butter Wouldn't Melt; Guilty 2; Guilty; Naughty But Nice (all drypoint).

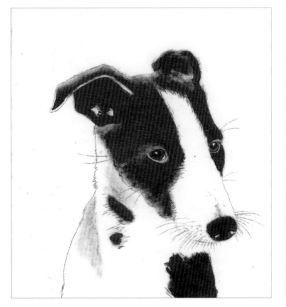

SONIA ROLLO

Sonia's interest in animals started in childhood with a pig called Hilary, geese called Charlie and Cassandra, and a mongrel, Pearl. Her current dog is the elderly Nipper, subject of the etching below.

She has been a dog lover all her life. Aged five, her first was a very independent fat black mongrel named Pearl. Nipper, her present muse, is named after the HMV dog. He has this year been to the Royal Academy Summer Exhibition under the pseudonym of Miss J. Russell – also the name of the print below.

Other dogs sketched and etched by the artist include those of her friends and sometimes of complete strangers. "Park walks with Nipper have provided me with lots of subjects for my dog etchings."

Sonia's early training as a biologist (she graduated from Glasgow University with a BSc in agricultural botany) meant observing plants and animals, drawing them to aid understanding. "But now I can have fun with my drawings and make them into etchings!

"The starting point is a simple line drawing of the animal. This allows me to study the form and muscle structure; to really look at the creature. For the etchings, I use carmine paper to transfer the drawing on to a zinc plate. The animal is then fleshed out by using aquatint techniques.

"To create the textures of fur or feather, I first cover the plate with soft wax, then scratch into the wax with various tools. These include wire brushes, a metal pan-scrub, a rough sponge or a studded wheel called a roulette. Nitric acid bites into the scratches to make grooves, which will hold the printing ink. The final act is to print the image on my Rochat press.

"The background of the image is minimal or non-existent to focus the viewer's gaze on the animal. You look at the animal, and the animal looks at you. The eyes have it...

"After more than 20 years of using the strange, complicated techniques of etching, I am still surprised by the characters of the animals that appear."

Many of Sonia's prints are inked 'à la poupée': also called 'dollying', this means that several colours are printed on the same plate at the same time.

Sonia is a founder member of Half Moon Printmakers (recently relocated to a new south-east London studio), a member of the cooperative Southbank Printmakers and a past vice-chair of the Printmakers' Council.
www.soniarollo.com

Facing page: Miss J. Russell (etching). Below left: You Clever Little Sausage (etching). Below right: Alfie (etching/collagraph).

*'Park walks with Nipper
have provided me with lots of subjects
for my dog etchings'*

*Left: Stan the Man. Top: Murdo, Margot and Morag. Above: The Love Light in Your Eyes 2
(all etchings by Sonia Rollo).*

SHELAGH CASEBOURNE

Berkshire-based Shelagh created 'Basil Sleeping' using a combination of a photographic screenprint and hand-cut stencils. "It's taken from a drawing of one of my Flat-coated Retrievers, Basil, in a characteristic, twisted pose that he often adopts when dozing. I liked the 'noise' left on the image from the photographic stencil, which was due to a grainy copy, but it's really the flat colour achieved by the stencils that draws me to screenprinting as a process."

Shelagh uses a variety of printmaking techniques including drypoint, linocut and screenprint. "Recently I have been experimenting with combining different processes, such as screenprinting and linocut, which produces some really interesting effects."

www.shelaghcasebourne.com

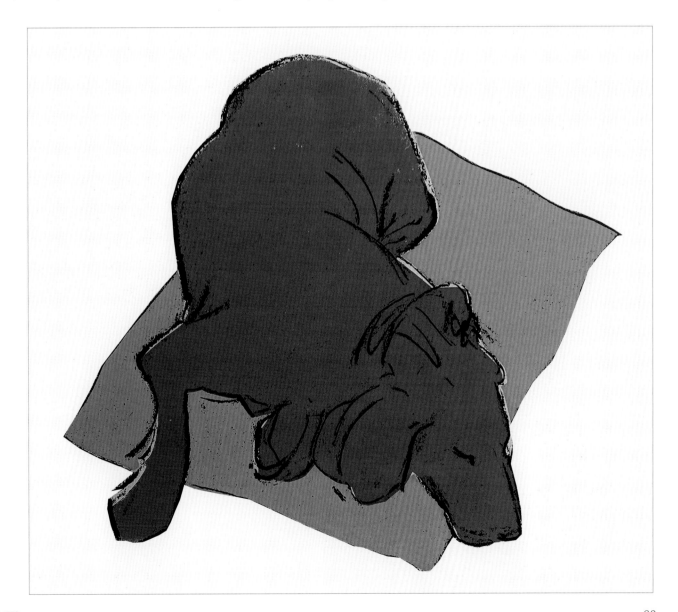

MARY COLLETT

Bristol-based Mary has immortalised in print a number of her dogs through the years, from Jazz and Robbie to current dog Bella.

"Jazz was a very gentle working Labrador, completely obsessed with retrieving balls or sticks. This was a study I did of her when she was an elderly dog, using etched lino and printed over grey paper [page 94]. I then added a gold leaf background so that it was like a dog version of an icon...

"We adopted Robbie when he was about three years old – by then he had spent quite a bit of his life in the dogs' home. He was probably a Labrador/Vizsla cross, and very handsome. He was a huge bundle of energy, needing constant company, and so he fitted in with Jazz and our two young children with ease. He chased bees, flies, wasps and even kites, which led to some embarrassing encounters on the Bristol Downs; he swam in

the sea after seagulls until he was a dot on the horizon and I had to hold back my 10-year-old daughter from going in to 'rescue' him. He somehow survived all his adventures until he was 15." The prints of Jazz and Robbie hang as a pair, so Mary also gave 'Robbie' (opposite, left) a gold leaf background

'Bella's Leap' (page 94) features Bella, "an adorable Labrador/Staffie cross whom we adopted at six months old. She is enormously

affectionate and needy (the Staffie side) as well as being hopelessly greedy (the Labrador side). In this print I hoped to capture a sense of movement and also some of Bella's joy and her enthusiasm for life."

Mary has also featured friends' dogs, such as 'Maddie' (page 92); and taken inspiration from particular canine features, as in 'Little Big Nosed Dog 1' (page 93) and 'Greyhound' (below right), "based on the wonderful *Galgos*, or Spanish Greyhounds, which have these extravagantly long noses – although I may have exaggerated the length a bit…".

Indeed, inspiration comes from a variety of sources. 'Bassett Hound' (far left) is the beginning of a series of prints Mary created to illustrate the seven deadly sins. "I decided that a dog would be the best candidate for 'envy' as they have such expressive eyes when pleading for food or attention. I chose a Basset Hound as they have such beautifully floppy, sad faces, and I also love the way their feet look like they've been put on slightly the wrong way round. Eventually, each print in the series incorporated an old bank note or cheque as a reference to money being the root of all evil [see page 7]."

From far left: Bassett Hound; The Eyes Have It 1 (both linocuts); Robbie; Greyhound (both etched lino). ▶

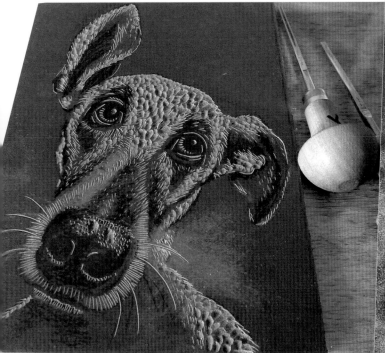

Facing page: Maddie (linocut). This page, top left: lino block for Little Big Nosed Dog 1 (linocut shown top right). Left: Jack (linocut). Page 94, top, far left: Life in the Old Dog 1 (linocut); middle: etched lino block for Jazz (etched linoprint shown far right). Bottom row, from left: Bella's Leap (etched lino); printing Bella's Leap.

The expressiveness of Jack Russells led to Mary's print 'Jack' (page 92). "Dogs are such good communicators, and I just love the way they often tip their heads on one side when listening to you. We have friends with Jack Russells, and they seem to be the best at achieving this cocked head look – which I hope I have captured in my print."

Finally, 'Life in the Old Dog 1' (page 94) was made for her father, who had been seriously ill in his mid-eighties but made a strong recovery against the odds. "I celebrated that by naming the print 'Life in the Old Dog' – and my father had a pretty impressive set of eyebrows, too!"

www.linoprints.co.uk ▶

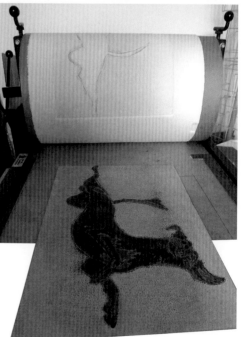

All images on this page: Mary Collett

AMIE HASLEN

Suffolk-based painter-printmaker Amie explains that Gemma, subject of her linocut Christmas card design on the right, is her and partner Charlie's four-year-old Sprockador (half Cocker Spaniel, quarter Labrador and quarter Springer Spaniel). "She is compact like a Spaniel but has Lab features so looks like a Lab puppy. She is a great companion and model in the studio, staying fast asleep for a long time. In this linocut she has a beaded collar which goes very well with the Christmassy colours of green and red.

"I decided to make a Saluki print because I find them interesting dogs. They have lovely long legs, silky ears and such elegant, serene faces. These graceful lines complement the formal garden but also contrast with the structural plants. I wanted this print to have an ethereal quality, so chose soft colours. It is a 4-block linocut, with a little added watercolour for the sky and the alliums. I graduated the colours on the roller so they were darker in the foreground, giving the garden a bit of distance. Lots of extender was used in the ink to give the colours more luminosity. *www.amiehaslen.com*

Below: Gemma. Bottom: Saluki and Garden (both linocuts).

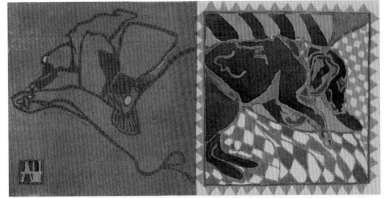

TERESA WINCHESTER

Teresa Winchester is a printmaker and also a storyteller with a great fascination for the natural world. "Living near Brighton there are plenty of opportunities to walk over the South Downs and to immerse yourself in open spaces and woods which can feed ideas and are a reminder of the tales you heard as a child.

"As well as being near the Downs, Brighton is also close to Gatwick and an opportunity to catch a plane to faraway places such as India, Japan, Africa and South America, all with rich environments and culture. Plenty there to inspire, draw and photograph.

"I've always liked to draw what I see around me, and have done so since I was a child. At times it becomes quite obsessional, and I now have many sketchbooks. These drawings sometimes become the inspiration for new prints, and that's true for my dog images here.

"This may come as a surprise, but I'm not at all happy around dogs. They're beautiful creatures, and I understand why people love them – but, sadly, I've had quite a few unlucky experiences with dogs that have made me very wary of being near them.

"Fortunately, one of my friends acquired a very calm and peaceful Lurcher. One perfect summer day we were lazing in her lovely garden with only the sound of the birds. Her dog was stretched out in a dozy dream on the daisy-covered grass, and it was the perfect chance to make a number of drawings. When I look at 'Dozy Dreamy Day' [top right, opposite] I can always recall that perfect afternoon with the gentle sun, the views across the Downs and the ever-present song of the blackbird.

"Being fascinated by stories, I didn't want to turn my drawings into simply dog portraits and so decided to create a narrative element that would get the viewer wondering what was happening in the image and then create their own story. Many times I've been asked about the dynamics between the dog and the rabbit. Are they at peace together or is something going to happen? I can't answer that!

Left: Finding the Bluebird. Above: Dog and Mice.
Top right: Dozy Dreamy Day. Right: Tree Jumping (all linocuts).

"Sometimes I've been told that I put 'opposites' into my prints. By that maybe people mean creatures that would not necessarily be comfortable in each other's company – such as the dog and the cat and the mice and the dog. I like to think that element contributes towards the story.

"Travelling is one of my passions, and it was on a trip to Madagascar that I met the little dog that became my print 'Dog and Mice' [above]. We were walking through a rather dilapidated village on a dull, rainy day and this little dog came wandering out of the hut. Fortunately there was time for a quick sketch and some photographs, and this dog became one of my most popular prints."

Teresa's linoprints are usually printed with two blocks and produced on an old Columbian press at the BIP studio in Brighton. They can be found in galleries throughout the country.

www.teresawinchester.co.uk

PAT SCHAVERIEN

One of Pat's earliest memories was of the family dog, Bimbo. "He was very fond of liquorice Catherine Wheels, his rubber ring and drooling at the dinner table! Half Boxer (hence the drooling) and half Alsatian (definitely loyal), he was very much loved in our household. As an adult, I have not owned or lived with a dog, but I still feel a strong connection – and, because of this, dogs have featured in some of my etchings.

"Often when I have been away on holiday, dogs seem to make an appearance. I found 'Red Setter' [page 100] on a beach in Southwold. 'Dachshund' [also page 100] was jumping madly up and down behind a gate, and 'Puppy' [below left] was seen waiting impatiently in a car for its owner to arrive."

Pat says she has always had an interest in photography, and she uses some of the photographs she has taken as a starting point for her prints. "Most of my etchings are 'sugar lift'. This is made by painting on the surface of a zinc plate with a brush dipped in a solution of Indian ink and sugar. The solution is eventually removed, or 'lifted', before the plate goes into the acid. After the sugar lifts, the aquatint is applied and acid bites into the portions that were drawn with the solution."

Pat studied printmaking at the Slade School of Art. Her work has been acquired by hospitals and museums (including the V&A and the Museum of London), and her greetings cards have been published worldwide. She has illustrated two books, *Weep Not For Me* by

Far left: Pug. Bottom, left to right: Puppy; Banshee; French Bulldog; Three Dogs. Below, left to right: Monty; Charlie; Tia (all etchings with aquatint).

*Left: Red Setter.
Facing page, clockwise
from top left:
Dachshund; Pico;
Tigger; Molly and
Becks (all etchings
with aquatint).*

Constance Jenkins (Souvenir Press, 1999), in memory of a beloved cat; and *Naming and Blessing* by Andrew Tawn (Souvenir Press, 2010), a book of name prayers. Her cat etchings also appeared in *The Printmaker's Cat* (the extended edition), published by Mascot Media in 2015.

www.printmakers3.com

DEBBIE KENDALL

Printmaker and hand-lettering artist Debbie hand prints art for those people who love dogs, inspired by her muse and companion, a Portuguese Water Dog named Figo.

"I use hand-lettered words and illustration to interpret the unique connection people have with their dogs. My lettering is deliberately idiosyncratic and wonky, and I often combine it with illustration and vintage decorative elements typical of 19th-century ephemera. I love the quirks and colloquialisms of the English language, with its curious idioms and turns of phrase, and enjoy finding ways that these can be incorporated into my prints."

Debbie does a lot of 'dog watching' – "observing how dogs react and adapt to life in a human world". A selection of her

Left: Rhyme of a Rescue Dog. Centre: In Dogs We Trust, framed, yellow colourway. Right: In Dogs We Trust, blue (all linocuts).

dog-themed work is shown here, including the linocuts 'Rhyme of a Rescue Dog' (below left) and 'In Dogs We Trust' (below centre and right). In the former linoprint, "all the dogs and letters of the poem were carved by hand (in reverse) into the two plates – one for each

colour – and hand-printed using an etching press. The print was inspired by the thousands of dogs in shelters who are waiting for their forever home. Taking the form of a poem, written by a rescued dog, it is a heartfelt 'ode of gratitude' to all those who have let

a rescue dog into their hearts and homes."

The 2-colour linoprint 'In Dogs We Trust' was created "to celebrate the unique and timeless bond between dogs and humans. A windswept, scruffy dog sits atop a globe as it whirls through space – a constant and

*Top left: Figo and printer's ink. Left: ink tubes. Above: inking
British Isles plate. Right: Dogs of the British Isles (linocut).*

reassuring companion as we forge ahead on life's ever-changing journey."

'Dogs of the British Isles' (above) is inspired by antique maps of the 18th and 19th centuries, and celebrates the many dog breeds that have originated in the British Isles. "Also depicted are some breeds (like the Greyhound) that, despite earlier origins in other countries, were developed into the breed standard that we know today in Britain. If a breed can be traced to a particular area, it is illustrated in that approximate geographical location on the map (eg, Norfolk Terrier in Norfolk); otherwise, breeds are evenly distributed throughout the map."

Each print in the edition was hand-printed from a lino plate. "The design is carved by hand into the lino using a series of gouges. Each line and dog and all the lettering are painstakingly carved out (in reverse so that they are the right way round when printed) – and, as each cut is final, there is no room for error. It took over 60 hours of carving to create this plate."

www.theenlightenedhound.com

TOR HILDYARD

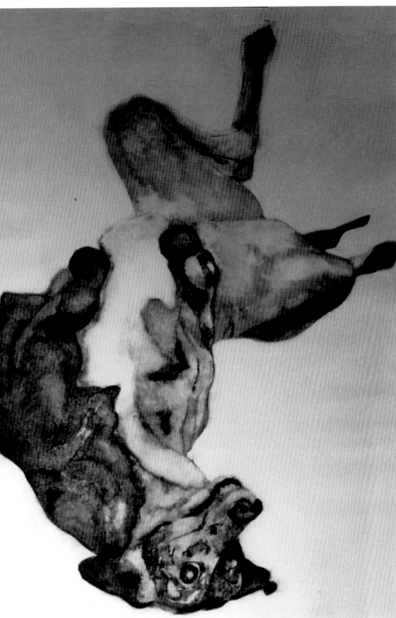

Dogs have played a very large part in Tor's adult life. "As a child I wasn't allowed one, so my idea of heaven was to go and stay with my Great Aunt, who had at least 15 dogs, ranging from Great Danes to Yorkshire Terriers.

"Once I left home there was no stopping me. My first canine companion was a naughty Spaniel called Chloe and now, eight dogs later, I have my loyal and elderly Inca."

When it comes to making prints of animals, Worcestershire-based Tor finds collagraphs a "wonderful medium for expressing exciting marks and textures", as seen in 'You're Joking' (far left, top) and 'Stretch' (left). Tor says she loves Basset Hounds' facial expressions, and the way Greyhounds "stretch out in gay abandonment". 'Innocence' and 'Mr Muscle' (overleaf) convey Spaniels' innate naughtiness and Bulldogs' strong character, respectively; while 'Bed' (also overleaf) features her friend's Greyhound, Eysor.

The different forms of etching can also be an exciting way of mark-making for animal prints, says Tor. "'Sweet Dreams' [far left, bottom] and 'Resting' [middle] are softground etchings with aquatint of my old dog, Peachy; while I was able to depict the feeling of speed in 'Racing II' [overleaf] by drawing directly on to the plate using an oil pastel.

"'Stretching Out' [overleaf] grew out of drawings of my friend's Dachshund/Chihuahua cross; while 'Right: Please!' [also overleaf] was one of a series showing the various expressions that dogs adopt to win humans round."

www.torhildyard.moonfruit.com

Top left: You're Joking (collagraph).
Bottom left: Sweet Dreams (etching).
Middle: Resting (etching).
Left: Stretch (collagraph). ▶

Left: Mr Muscle (collagraph).
Top: Stretching Out (etching).
Above: Innocence (collagraph).
Right: Please! (etching).
Far right, top and bottom: Bed
(collagraph); Racing II (etching).

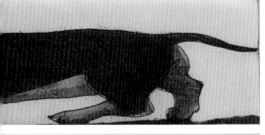

VICTORIA KEEBLE

Over the years Victoria has collected many pictures of dogs in her scrapbooks and drawn them in her sketchbooks so that she has a reminder of their shapes, quirks and movements.

"As a child I was taken to numerous dog shows as my mother bred Pugs, so I used to wander around looking at the different breeds on their benches. Along with cats and horses, dogs have featured in my work since an early age. Dogs have a 'joie de vivre' that is very appealing.

"'Stars and Stripes' [below left], 'Circus Horse' [top, far right] and 'Hoop-la' [top, near right] depict stylized Bull Terriers, a breed that I grew up with. 'Juggler' [below right] features terriers and Dachshunds, as well as some other rather nondescript dogs."

Some of Victoria's animal prints, such as 'Pwyll's Hounds' (facing page, bottom right) and 'St Mellangell and the Hare' (facing page, bottom left), are inspired by Celtic folklore.

"Pwyll Pen Annwn was Prince of Dyfed and features in the medieval legendary tales of *Mabinogion*, the Welsh classic. Melangell, the daughter of an Irish king, went to Powys in central Wales to become a hermit; she lived a peaceful, solitary life until the Prince of Powys, Brochwel Ysgithrog, went hunting and frightened a hare that took refuge under Melangell's cloak. The Prince's dogs were subdued and, deeply impressed, he gave her the valley in which to create a sanctuary. Ever since, Pennant Melangell has been a place of pilgrimage; and St Melangell remains the patron saint of hares, rabbits, small animals and the natural environment."

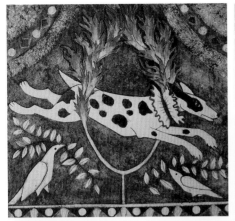

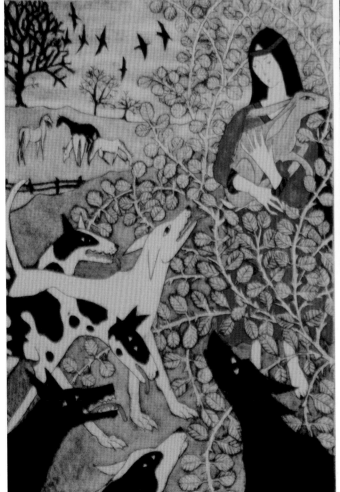

Facing page, from left: Stars and Stripes; Juggler. This page, clockwise from top left: Hoop-la;
Snap Dog; Circus Horse; Pwyll's Hounds; St Melangell and the Hare (all collagraphs).

'Snap-Dog' (top centre) is based on a Whippet, "such a graceful, sinuous, decorative creature. Miners called the Whippet 'snap-dog' because of its lightning acceleration when setting off in pursuit of rabbits."

Victoria originally trained and worked as a textile designer, before studying printmaking at Hereford College of Art. "I was instantly hooked, and at last felt I could let my imagination run wild, something that was certainly not encouraged at art school in the late 1950s!"

Although she works in several print media, her preference is collagraph. She is a member of the Hay Makers, a co-operative of local designer-makers in Hay-on-Wye; and her work is in private collections throughout the world.

www.victoria-keeble.com

BARBARA BARLOW

Cheshire-based artist Barbara creates a wide range of reduction linocuts, but domestic and wild animals and birds are a particular passion. "I discovered wonderful challenges trying to depict fur, hair, wool, feather, etc, using the medium of linocut."

Many of Barbara's prints feature family pets, and other dogs met locally and abroad on holiday. 'Companions' (below left) shows her niece Lois's Inuit dog, Anik, watching over baby Artie J; 'Sleeping Beauties' (below right) captures Lois and Anik asleep together; and 'Anik Meets a Friend' (bottom left, opposite) is based on a canine encounter when Anik visited the dog breeder who reared her.

"Anik is a loyal dog who follows her owner from room to room and keeps a constant eye on her and on her two children, Artie J and Jesse. I think maybe sometimes Anik gets a little anxious for her family!

"The other dog in 'Anik Meets a Friend' is a dark example of the breed. I wanted the background to highlight the contrast between them, so I invented a diagonal lace edge splitting the backdrop and hoped that the way I positioned their faces and bodies demonstrated their interest in each other."

'Happy Dogs' (top left, opposite) was inspired by dogs encountered while Barbara was holidaying on the Greek island of Skiathos.

"The owner of our rental property had four dogs, and two of them virtually lived with us during our stay. We love dogs; and, not having any of our own, we were thrilled with this temporary arrangement – it was partly why we returned the following year." Barbara featured their beagle, Guiseppe, on two different occasions. Top left opposite shows him in three positions. "He was self-contained and hard to read but clearly a happy and contented dog. The strong light and shade reflect the hot,

Below left and right: Companions; Sleeping Beauties. Opposite, clockwise from top left: Happy Dogs; Guiseppe; What a Whippet; Anik Meets a Friend (all linocuts).

bright climate; and the ground depicts the crazy paving path that he walked along to reach our temporary abode."

Back home, Barbara was driving through her village when she noticed a dog event in a nearby field. "I went home to fetch my camera, returned to the field and asked dog owners their permission to photograph their pets. The Whippet has a long face and neck, and I sought to exaggerate these characteristics in my resulting print, 'What a Whippet!' [page 113]. I thought the subject might suit a pop art approach like Roy Lichtenstein's Whaam! and, having shown it at exhibitions, it does sometimes make people guffaw. It certainly did when I showed it on Facebook!"

The three dogs in 'Bearded Collies' (top left and right) belonged to the chair of the Bearded Collie Club, and Barbara wanted to highlight the way dogs of this breed can barely see through their fringe – "so, typically, you see two dark buttons staring at you through a mass of hair" – and their tendency to pant.

Finally, 'Resting' (bottom left) is a memorial to Frodo, who belonged to her niece. "He led a long and happy life, but when he died Lois was heartbroken. He is shown peacefully lying down underneath the moon."

email: barbarajohnbarlow@gmail.com

Top left and right: Bearded Collies.
Left: Resting (all linocuts by Barbara Barlow).

AMANDA AVERILLO

Kent-based painter-printmaker Amanda works in the painterly monoprinting medium to make one-off images of dramatic, light-filled seascapes.

"The monoprint on the right was inspired by a photo I took at Camber Sands of a group of dogs joyfully running into the sea. There were lots of dogs at Camber that day with their owners, and I think these and another two were all being walked by one lady!

"The dogs in the print below right are called Riley and Tess, and belonged to a friend of mine called Dave Yarrington who commissioned me to make a print of him and his beloved Labradors. Riley and Tess were elderly when I made the print, and are now sadly no longer with us.

"I studied Fine Art and Printmaking at Hertfordshire College of Art and Design, and at Croydon Art College in the 1980s. In 2001 I moved to the beautiful Kent countryside from London and set up a printmaking workshop teaching the techniques to adults, and at the same time creating my own work to exhibit.

"I still run my classes from my garden studio in Sissinghurst and I now mainly make monoprints inspired by the beautiful coastline around East Sussex. I aim to capture the wonderful light and life around the sea shore."

Two of Amanda's pupils have contributed work to this book, namely Sue Clements (page 39) and Cyril Vickers (page 168).

www.amandaaverilloart.com

Top: 5 Go Mad at the Coast.
Right: Dogs' Play (both monoprints).

NICK WONHAM

The subject matter of illustrator and printmaker Nick's art often derives from his love of nature and animals, but he is also inspired by fairy tales, nursery rhymes and poetry.

"'All the Dogs' [opposite, left] is an illustration for a horrible nursery rhyme – more of a playground chant, really:

Tell tale tit!
Your tongue shall be slit,
And all the dogs in the town
Shall have a little bit.

"'Jumping Dog' [page 4] and 'Hark, Hark' [page 3] are also nursery rhyme illustrations, all three of which are from my book *Red Herrings* (Incline Press), a selection of animal-themed nursery rhymes illustrated with linocuts."

Nick's 'Dotty Dog' reduction vinyl cut (below) was created especially for sale in The Dotty Dog Gallery in Shrewsbury. "Not that it was a commission, but once I had the idea of a Dalmatian in the snow I couldn't resist making the print. In truth, it was only later, when I watched it for the first time with my children, that I realised that Disney had the idea long

before me in the snowy scene in *One Hundred and One Dalmatians*!"

'Dachshund' (top right) was also a commission, a present for Nick's sister-in-law from her partner. "She loves 'sausage dogs' and had one called Dingle when she was a teenager. When Dingle's back legs gave up as she got older, she was carried around in her basket like The Queen of Sheba.

"'Jack Russell' [bottom right] was made as a partner to 'Dachshund' for an exhibition; while 'Fox Terrier' [which appears on the front cover] was created especially with my wife in mind as she loves Fox Terriers."

www.nickwonham.com

Facing page, top: Schnauzer; bottom: Dotty Dog (both vinyl cuts). Above: All The Dogs (linocut). Top right: Dachshund (vinyl cut). Right: Jack Russell (vinyl cut). Nick's 'Fox Terrier' vinyl cut appears on the front cover. Freedom! (vinyl cut); Hark, Hark (linocut); and Jumping Dog (linocut) appear on pages 2, 3 and 4.

BEVERLEY WHITE

B everley is of the opinion that dogs make excellent companions for sketching trips, providing both friendship and entertainment.

"Although a couple of my canine companions, Badger and Jack, both Collies, were not the easiest of dogs to go walking with, their loyalty was immense. Bertie, another rescue Collie, came with lots of problems for a very young dog; and, very upsettingly, died within eight months."

Badger is immortalised in 'Collie Dog' (above); Jack in 'Young Jack' (page 120); and Bertie in 'Find It!' (left), 'Let 'im Lie' and 'That'll Do' (both page 120).

"Collie ownership then gave way to terrier ownership. Robbie [the subject of 'Patterdale at High Water', opposite, and 'Anything Could Happen, page 120] was an

*'Dogs make excellent companions
for sketching trips, providing both
friendship and entertainment'*

*Facing page, bottom: Find It!
(linocut); top: Collie Dog (wood
engraving). Right: Patterdale at
High Water (linocut).*

elderly gentleman, his only weakness being a fondness for chasing chickens. However, he was an angel with the cat, so friendly that they often shared the same chair.

"Two years ago Mr Khan, a Bedlington cross, moved in. He is the colour of dry mud; and, though not a young dog (he is 10), he does gambol like a lamb around the saltmarsh where we live." Khan is often by Beverley's side when on duty in her gallery, and is the subject of 'Mop Head' (top right).

Beverley is a member of the Witherslack Artists & Makers Group and of the Lake Artists Society. She also helps run The Beach Hut Gallery, an artists' co-operative based at Kents Bank railway station on the shores of Morecambe Bay. *www.thebeachhutgallery.co.uk*

Clockwise from top left: Young Jack (wood engraving); Mop Head (linocut); Anything Could Happen; Let 'im Lie; That'll Do (all wood engravings by Beverley White).

Afer spending the majority of her working life lecturing in Surface Design for the University of The Arts, London, Drusilla took early retirement in 2009 and moved to Bishop's Castle, Shropshire. Since then, she has enjoyed exploring various forms of printmaking, settling on linocuts and collagraphs as her methods of choice.

'Luna' (right) is an example of the former medium, and is a beautiful Dalmatian belonging to one of Drusilla's friends. "Here she is sitting very comfortably on a sofa. I love the combination of spots and stripes, and had fun cutting them."

Drusilla also occasionally produces woodcuts, as with 'Rosie, the Harlequin Great Dane' (below). "Rosie was a beautiful Great Dane I met several years ago while walking on Bury Ditches hill fort. She was such a beautiful, gentle giant of a dog, with a very sad back story, that my heart went out to her and I asked to take her photo. Later I carved this woodcut of her from 4mm birch-faced plywood."

Drusilla has written four books of her own: *1000 Patterns* (A & C Black); and *Patterns, New Surface Design*; *Textiles Now*; and *The Pattern Sourcebook: a Century of Surface Design* (all Laurence King).

www.drusillacole.co.uk

Top: Luna (linocut).
Right: Rosie, the Harlequin Great Dane (woodcut).

ANN BRIDGES

For Kent-based painter-printmaker Ann Bridges, observational drawing is the starting point for her paintings and original prints.

"Dillon [immortalised here in three unique monoprints] was my daughter's dog, a mix of Collie and Springer Spaniel. When we lived in Wales I used to take him for long walks in and around the little village of Llanfair Dyffryn Clwyd. He features on many pages of my sketchbooks. No longer with us, the pictures remind us of his boundless energy."

Ann studied Illustration at Yale College (Coleg Cambria) and the North Wales College of Art and Design (Glyndwr University), graduating with First Class Honours in Design. A two-year placement at Chester Zoological Gardens as Artist in Residence provided her with her first studio and the opportunity to develop and broaden her practice.

She has been awarded Arts Council funding for research projects carried out through visual diaries and sketchbooks, and is a member of the Royal Cambrian Academy.

www.ann-bridges.com

Above: Dillon in the Woods in Spring. Left: Dillon in the Bluebell Wood. Facing page: Dillon in the Buttercup Field (all stencil-based monoprints).

'Dillon was a mix of Collie and Springer Spaniel, and these pictures remind us of his boundless energy'

KATHERINE PARKER

Clockwise from top left: Sula, Whippet; Kwela, working Cocker Spaniel; Harriet, Springer Spaniel; Lily, Labrador (all etchings).

The dogs behind Katherine's prints vary greatly in pedigree, size and temperament. "What they all have in common is that they are loved by their owners and are very much part of the family group.

"Most dog-owners will probably agree that once you have a dog your life changes for the better. There is a good reason why dogs are used for many kinds of therapy."

Katherine uses the traditional printmaking techniques of etching on zinc with hard ground and aquatint. She undertakes commissions of clients' animals and pets; and produces and sells other prints, mostly concerned with the natural world.

She has taken part in group exhibitions in London, and runs art clubs at several schools in the capital.

www.katherineparker.co.uk

'Most dog-owners will probably agree that once you have a dog your life changes for the better. There is a good reason why dogs are used for many kinds of therapy'

Clockwise from top left: Piper, Labrador; Guido, Labrador; CB, Soft-coated Wheaten Terrier; Winnie, Long-haired Miniature Dachshund; Zola, working Cocker Spaniel (all etchings).

SARAH BAYS

The start of Sarah's printmaking coincided with the arrival of Miniature Schnauzer Oscar, and so he became the star of some of her earliest prints. He has continued to feature occasionally ever since.

"I think it's safe to say he is what is often referred to as a character, and definitely the 'not always well-behaved dog' mentioned in my bio! Aged 12, he is now completely deaf and his sight is getting worse, but he is still very lively.

"'I Don't Believe We've Been Introduced'

[opposite page, far right] depicts his fascination for cows and their interest in him. A short period of calm – sniffing nose to nose through a fence or gate – is cut short abruptly when he lets out a sudden bark and watches them scatter in all directions. If he could snigger I'm sure he would.

"He got his comeuppance recently when, having sneaked into the field adjoining my parents' garden, he found himself chased by the entire herd.

"Oscar is not always at his best with other

dogs but found a friend in Freddie, who is depicted in 'Chase Me' [opposite page, below left]. The two of them spent a happy and noisy afternoon running – at full pelt, barking – around the house and garden until they were both exhausted.

"'He's Behind You' [below left] and 'Blissful Ignorance' [opposite page, bottom right] are based on sketches I did of Oscar while we were on holiday in Aldeburgh in Suffolk.

"There is also a cameo appearance from the cat who nearly came on holiday with us, having jumped into the car boot while we were packing! The same cat often appears at the window while I'm working – unobserved by Oscar, who would be incensed if he knew.

"'Let Him Lie' [opposite page, top], inspired by a Rembrandt etching and drypoint called 'Sleeping Puppy', is Oscar at rest. Needless to say, his usual resting place is the sofa where he snores gently, dreaming of cows perhaps…"

Sarah lives in Norwich, and produces prints from a small etching press on a tea trolley in the corner of her dining room. "I find my inspiration in my surroundings: the Norfolk countryside, its wildlife, birds, farm animals and coast. I am often inspired by my morning dog walks, the pattern of light through the trees and the shadows cast by the morning sun – and, of course, holidays provide further sources of inspiration in new surroundings."

www.sarahbays.co.uk

Facing page: top – Let Him Lie; bottom left: Chase Me (both drypoint);
bottom right: Blissful Ignorance (linocut).
Above left: He's Behind You (drypoint and linocut).
Above right: I Don't Believe We've Been Introduced (drypoint).

SHELLY PERKINS

S helly uses a mix of traditional and digital techniques to make her unusual and highly textural prints. Starting with detailed line drawings, painted washes and textures, she scans her hand-rendered work into the computer and overlays these elements to create multi-layered, digital collages.

In 'Hot House Hounds' (left) Shelly places her Irish Wolfhounds in a stately home setting, inspired by Stubbs. "I liked the idea of these gentle giants being set inside a traditional 'hot house', where exotic fruits would have been grown from the 16th century onwards to impress important guests. The vibrant orange of the fruits, coupled with the lovely soft greys of the dogs' coats, makes for an irresistible contrast."

'Coursers Court' (top) features two charismatic dogs, Chloe and Rio. "Chloe was a Greyhound who was possibly used for hare-coursing before ending up at a rescue centre. Her companion, the Lurcher Rio, was placed with her, and Chloe's gentle demeanour was the perfect antidote to Rio's anxiety. The pair stayed together, becoming great friends and getting up to mischief – including racing around. But once their exercise fix was over, they loved nothing more than crashing out on the sofa."

Shelly embraces a touch of the exotic with her highly threatened 'African Hunting Dogs' (right) inspired by a recent field trip to South Luangwa in Zambia. "I was extremely lucky to get to spend an hour sketching them from our safari vehicle."

www.shellyperkins.co.uk

Left: Hot House Hounds. Top: Coursers Court. Right: African Hunting Dogs (all digital collage prints from hand-drawn originals).

PHILLIP KINGSBURY

Phillip, a printmaker/ graphic designer based in Wiltshire, uses a wooden spoon to create his linoprints (hence his website name!), and enjoys experimenting with colour and texture.

"While I was at art college I worked with lots of media and tried different types of printing: linocut was my favourite, particularly the reduction technique. With some work, I have also experimented with digitally added colour – it's intriguing to mix a traditional printing technique such as lino with modern technology."

The linocuts featured here were printed using Caligo ink on a Rollaco Press, and were all commissions. "Some clients like to have a portrait of their dogs, while others like to portray them out and about on their favourite walks."

www.woodenspoonpress.com

Left: Dog Walkers. Above: Dog in Blue.
Top right: River Walk.
Right: Dog (all linocuts).

GILL MUNN

Gill, who is based in Norfolk, has worked as a designer, corporate film-maker, illustrator, educator of both children and adults – and, more recently, as an artist and experimental printmaker.

She works in drypoint when the image requires draughtsmanship; and in collagraph when she wants to capture a mood or feeling, finding that the combination of line, colour, texture and invention often leads to "a completely random, unexpected outcome".

All of the prints shown here feature one very special dog. "Daisy is a white and tan Jack Russell of unknown parentage (she came to us via The Dogs Trust as a puppy).

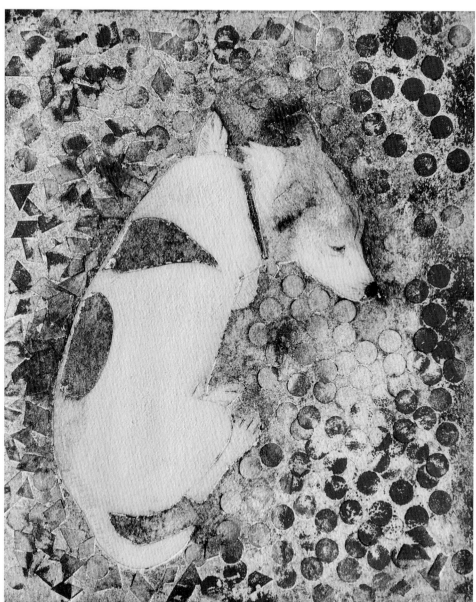

Like most 'Jacks', she may be small, but she has a huge personality and is very skilled at making us humans do exactly what she wants. She has very expressive ears, soulful eyes and a comical toothy grin with which she greets visitors – all of which make her a great subject, if only she would stay still for more than two minutes!

"I have countless quick, unfinished sketches, and my prints often rely on imagination as much as on observation.

"I am still working on creating the print that completely captures Daisy, but it is a most delightful work in progress…"

www.gillmunnart.co.uk

Far left: Flower-bed (collagraph). Above left: Hang-dog (drypoint). Left: Star (hand-coloured drypoint). Right: Dog Days of Summer (collagraph).

GEORGINA WARNE

Georgina is a gifted Norfolk-based ceramicist and printmaker who combines both practices, often printing directly on to clay. Many of her drypoint prints and etchings are tinted with watercolour, but she also produces charming linocuts often steeped in mythology.

Hares have been a constant theme in her work (Georgina made a spectacular contribution to our book *The Artful Hare*), and 'The Winter Hare' (below centre) shows a hare turning the tables on a hare-coursing dog.

Black Shuck – the ghostly hound said to roam the coastline and countryside of East Anglia – is the inspiration for the other three prints shown here, 'Lonely Shuck' (far left), 'Night Time Hunters' (right) and 'Black Shuck and Friend' (below) – the latter based on the

artist's dear departed dog Boris, described by Georgina as "a bit of a Black Shuck".

Georgina studied Ceramics and Glass at Birmingham Institute of Art and Design, and did her MA in Ceramics at Cardiff School of Art and Design. She has run workshops on ceramics and printmaking in community groups and schools, as well as leading out-reach projects with bodies such as The National Trust.

www.georginawarne.co.uk

Far left: Lonely Shuck (drypoint). Bottom centre: The Winter Hare (linocut). Top centre: Black Shuck and Friend (linocut). Below right: Night Time Hunters (drypoint and watercolour).

CAROLINE BARKER

Devon-based Caroline is part of the Press Gang Printmakers co-operative, which meets at the Loft Studio in Salcombe. She particularly enjoys the natural world, and this is reflected in most of her work.

Caroline likes to use the collagraph technique for intaglio prints to produce work that is full of texture; but also makes layered relief prints from linocuts, as well as combining both these techniques with drypoint etching.

'Bearded Friend' (left) features Lotte, her brother's Miniature Schnauzer. "She is extremely well behaved, so much so that she is a Pets as Therapy (PAT) dog and is taken into schools and nursing homes to help comfort people who are struggling.

"Her colour is 'pepper and salt', and I thought a collagraph would be a great technique to use to bring out her amazing fur with wonderful eyebrows and beard. I tried hard to convey her character in this print.

"I love the doleful look of most Lurchers. A friend of mine walked into the gallery where I was stewarding with her Lurcher cross, so I had plenty of time to observe her and take some photos. I drew her first [see sketch below] and then made the collagraph plate [for the print, 'Anticipation', below left]. I like to respond quickly to a subject before I lose the mood and feel of what I have observed."

www.carolinebarkerart.co.uk

Top left: Bearded Friend (collagraph).
Bottom left: Anticipation (collagraph).
Below: pencil drawing for Anticipation.

ISABEL HUTCHISON

The King Charles Spaniels depicted here were once Isabel's next-door neighbours. "The sulky little dog who is the subject of 'Socks' [bottom] was briefly my charge as I baby-sat him for a whole week when he was just a little puppy. As an artist sitting at my easel, I had to work with him on my lap – he wanted my undivided attention. He was very sweet, and very spoilt, and when he didn't get his way he would adopt the expression captured in the etching that indicated you were supposed to understand and get what he meant.

"Eventually the little dog grew up and got a companion, another King Charles, who was quite a spunky little fellow by comparison. Of course, 'Socks and Raffles' [right] had to be captured together languishing in their big dog bed."

Isabel is based in London and Hampshire, and takes much of her inspiration from animals and the natural world. Her work has been published in books and as greetings cards, and she exhibits through galleries and mixed shows.

www.izzyhutchison.com

'Socks was very sweet, and very spoilt, and when he didn't get his way he would adopt an expression that indicated you were supposed to understand and get what he meant'

Top: Socks and Raffles.
Right: Socks (both etchings).

GLORIA DEAN

Gloria grew up on her grandparents' farm in north Norfolk, where she enjoyed an idyllic childhood. Her interest in art began very early, and as a child she would draw and scribble on anything that came to hand.

Her career as an artist began during the late 1970s when she opened a small art gallery, representing her own and other artists' work. Since then her work has spanned sculpture, book illustration, stage sets, furniture decoration and restoration – and printmaking.

Animals feature strongly in her work. "I have always loved hounds of all types, and have been privileged to count many as my friends over the years. Their gentleness, and the iconic clean lines, give them an ethereal quality, lending themselves to art.

"Inspired by these qualities, I did not want to produce fussy drawings or blocks but strive to keep the lines pure and simple. Lino is perfect for this, and I often cut straight on to the block without pre-drawing. I use a bamboo baren and hand-press on to a variety of Japanese and other handmade papers."

'Grace and Loyalty' (left) is inspired by Gloria's many rescued Greyhounds – "they rest their heads so quietly in hands or on laps. Their grace and loyalty to each other and to their owners inspired my print of the same name."

'Quiver' (far right) features

*'Rescued Greyhounds rest their heads so quietly
in hands or on laps, and show such grace
and loyalty to each other and to their owners'*

her friends' "beautiful little Whippet by the same name"; while 'Winter Walk' (below left) shows a lady walking two Borzois as the snow falls and the wind blows – she is dressed to match the drama of the two hounds. 'Home and Dry' (overleaf) also features two Borzois at home by the fire, their flowing lines contrasting with the rigid structure of architecture.

Gloria's work is held in private collections worldwide.

www.gloriadean.com

*Opposite: Grace and Loyalty.
Below left: Winter Walk.
Below right: Quiver (all linocuts).*

Home and Dry (linocut by Gloria Dean).

GILLIAN GOLDING

Specialising in etchings, linocuts and, more recently, lithographs and screenprints, Gillian divides her time between London (where she works in the printmaking department at Goldsmith's College) and south-west France (where she is a member of Pierre Presse, a lithography atelier). She exhibits her work widely, both in the UK and abroad; and it is held in many private collections.

The journalist Fiona Graham-Mackay, in her review of the 2011 Royal Academy Summer Show for cultural website TMR, picked out Gillian's 'Morandi's Dog' as one of the highlights.

The print, shown below, is a homage to Italian painter and printmaker Giorgio Morandi (1890-1964). Inspired by Rembrandt, etching played a significant part in his artistic practice from the outset. Gillian uses the hatching and cross-hatching technique that is so typical of Morandi's work.

www.gilliangolding.co.uk

CHRIS SINDEN

Left: Expectation. Below: Blue Bed. Far right: New Collar. Bottom right: Dirty Habits No 2 (all linocuts).

After 30 years as an advertising art director, redundancy convinced Chris that it was time for a career change. A move to Norway (and back) brought with it a love of linocutting; and, having come to the art late in life, he set out to find a style that would set his work apart.

"Since those early experimental days I have developed a style where smaller images butt up to make the larger final picture. Utilising both printmaking techniques (one block, one colour and reduction printing), using slightly unmatched colours and details and often to an irregular format, most of my linocuts take on a collage appearance. Although these take a long time to plan and print, I enjoy the challenge of working in this complicated way."

"The print 'Expectation' [far left] shows my youngest daughter's Sussex Spaniel Riley during puppy training. 'New Collar' [right] is a portrait of my eldest daughter's Cockapoo Phoebe. 'Blue Bed' [left] is a study of my ex-wife's brown Springer Spaniel Harvey.

"My 'Dirty Habits No 2' [below] belongs to a humorous series of linocuts made while I was trying to earn a living in Norway.

"As a child we had a Beagle as the family pet. When my own children were youngsters we bought a West Highland Terrier. With white hair and a white beard I have now fulfilled the popular observation that owners look like their dogs!"

www.sindencox-art.co.uk

HAZEL McNAB

Hazel explains that Izzy, the eight-year-old working Labrador depicted here, is something of a tomboy.

"The lucky girl lives near a beach in Cornwall. Life is good for this beach baby; and if she's not exploring the coastal paths she's racing down the beach to swim in the sea.

"I was inspired by the shadows she created on the sand, and love the simplicity of these prints."

Hazel studied Fashion and Textiles at St Martins School of Art in London, and has always been intrigued by capturing colours, textures and patterns. "Living in the beautiful Shropshire countryside, I'm inspired by nature and its changing seasons." *www.hazelmcnab.com*

Left: Izzy 2. Right: Izzy 1 (both reduction linocuts). Izzy linocuts also appear on page 3 and on the front cover.

JAMES GREEN

Sheffield-based artist/printmaker James Green specialises in linocut prints, with subjects ranging from people and animals to landscapes and the absurd. "I'm very much drawn to the physicality of the printing process, the unpredictable nature of the materials, and the decisions you have to take when composing a linocut print."

'Woody' (below) is a linocut/screenprint, featuring a Collie-cross that belongs to friends of James from Bristol. "I was rather taken by the faraway look he always had in his eyes, so endeavoured to try and capture this in my print." 'Olive The Whippet' (below left) is a two-colour linocut print and was inspired by a dog that other friends were looking after for the weekend. "She seemed to have made a very comfy nest for herself in their house and was looking at me as if to say, 'I really hope you're not thinking of moving me'. I didn't. I had quite a challenge working out the foreground and background patterns, and the Whippet in the middle, and making sure that she stood out between them."

http://jamesgreenprintworks.blogspot.co.uk

Below left: Olive the Whippet (linocut).
Below right: Woody (linocut/screenprint).

LOUISE THOMPSON

Devon printmaker Louise Thompson often walks on Woolacombe Beach with her eight-year-old working Cocker Spaniel, Oscar – "invariably, he chases the gulls and makes them fly".

Oscar also comes with her to work at The Old Schoolroom Craft Gallery in Lee every day. "The collagraph print [below right] came about after doing an ink drawing of his face. I cut into cardboard with a scalpel, and inked it up with different coloured etching inks. Officially, he has lemon and white colouring, so I used yellow ochre but then also experimented with burnt umber.

"Archie [below left] belongs to my sister's family, and is a Goldendoodle, a cross between a Golden Retriever and a Poodle. This print, which I created as a gift for them, was fun to do. I wanted to keep the linocut marks used to depict his fur simple, so just printed it in dark grey and allowed the white paper to create texture."

Louise graduated from Falmouth School of Art with a degree in Fine Art, specialising in printmaking. Her preferred media are reduction cut linoprints and collagraphs, and she has recently started to experiment with solarplate etching. "I am excited by the possibility of working from ink drawings on acetate and then being able to etch and print from these."

email: louthompsonba@outlook.com

Left: Archie (linocut).
Right: Oscar (collagraph).

KAZ JONES

Kaz is self-taught, and began her artistic career with painting before introducing printmaking – linoprint, drypoint/ metalplate etching and wood engraving – into her practice.

"I find enormous pleasure in strong monochrome contrasts; and having the ability to take an everyday image and imbue it with a darker, brooding atmosphere just by the use of black ink is endlessly fascinating to me."

'Woof' (below) is a wood engraving of "a good boy's sniffer"; while 'Tigger by the Sea' (below right), an 8-colour reduction linoprint, is a portrait of "a lovely old gentleman of a dog who belongs to friends of mine in Ceredigion".

The stages in the making of the prints shown here demonstrate the skill involved in the process.

www.kazjonesart.co.uk

Opposite page, bottom: Woof (wood engraving); and, above, the block before the first inking. This page, bottom: Tigger by the Sea (linocut); and, right, the linoblock at the final layer stage.

HELEN D MOORE

Clockwise from below left: Hound Dog 2; Daydreamer 1; Cute Canine; Daydreamer 2 (all etchings). Facing page, left and right: Stargazing (collagraph); Winged Canine (etching).

Helen says she has always loved dogs as she grew up with them – "Dinky, Bunty, Trixie and Kimberlina of Oakmere – so my etchings naturally took a turn towards old canine companions.

"My etchings are all quite comical interpretations of photographs of dogs I take on my travels and dogs from my memory re-imagined. I have a large repertoire of etchings of

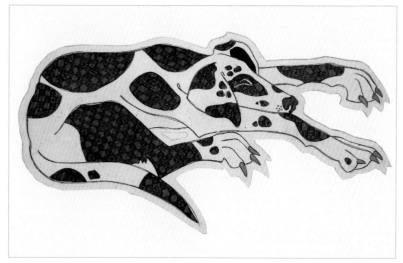

animals and birds, but my dog prints are some of my favourites. I enjoy making etching plates as I did my degree in jewellery design – and so a large piece of metal does not faze me! I fill my images full of patterns and use the process of cutting out my plates so that the shapes of the animals are embossed into the paper – as it is soaked before it is printed on and is therefore soft and malleable. I also like to over-etch lines and patterns and let the paper get pushed into these as it goes through the printing press. This causes patterns to stand out in relief on the finished prints.

"I think that eyes are very important on the faces of my creations, so I over-emphasise them – making them, and often the paws, bigger to make the viewer smile when they look at my images.

"I have never had my own dog, but hope to have one soon…"

www.helendmoore.co.uk

IAN MOWFORTH

Clockwise from top left: Basil the Wirehaired Pointing Griffon; Jason, the Australian Cattle Dog; Wilf the Whippet; Bruno the Boxer; Maggie, the English Bulldog (all linocuts). Facing page, clockwise from top left: Cyril the Corgi (blue version — black version on back cover); Woolfy the Wolfhound; Daisy the Weimaraner. Tita Petita the Chihuahua appears on page 3. Brenda the Bearded Collie appears on page 6 (all linocuts).

London-based Ian finds that lino is the most effective medium for representing the physical quality of a dog's coat; so, although he also enjoys etching, drypoint and lithography, all the prints shown here are linocuts.

"I play around with scale as I'm interested in the mark-making possibilities of the material. I print on to Japanese papers or Zerkall smooth. I never use black ink, but a mix of Prussian blue and Burnt umber. Sometimes I print just in blue or gold.

"I started painting dogs as a friend has a terrier and I wanted to make her a Christmas present. That was in 2014. I had a linocut of the same terrier, Princess, a rescue dog, in the RA summer show in 2017, and they made it into a card for the shop. It's still doing very well!

"I choose the subjects due to their physical presence. My goal is to capture the life of the dog as the image will outlive the animal."

Ian, who has an MA in Print from Brighton University, says that if he were a dog he'd be a Shih Tzu! *www.ianmowforth.com*

GILL BEDSON

Left: Bill Watching a Lamb (drypoint). Bottom left: Dog on a Sofa (reduction woodcut with lace). Below: Dog Encounters (both drypoint etchings). Facing page, left and right: Chester on a Sofa (woodcut); Bickerton Looking at a Butterfly (woodcut/chine-collé).

Suffolk printmaker Gill lives on a smallholding and keeps goats, pigs, sheep and chickens – "not to mention my two dogs, Bill and Titch". She enjoys immortalising in print her own dogs, those of friends, and others she meets when out and about.

"A dog on a sofa is one of my favourite things – it's the humour of a dog taking the place of a human that amuses me, and the battles some folk have trying to instil some sort of order with their four-legged friend.

"The 'Dog on a Sofa' reduction woodcut [far left, bottom] shows my friend's dog. We had many poses to choose from, but I love the luxuriousness of this set-up for a dog. The print has five layers of colour, and the cover on the left of the sofa was made using lace."

Closer to home, Bill provided the inspiration for 'Bill Watching a Lamb' (far left, top). "He loves to sit and view the field from the garden, especially when my sheep are in residence. On this particular day he was watching the lambs, and one of the lambs was watching him. Bill is leaning forward slightly as if ready to pounce! This print is made from a drypoint etching, and was a real challenge to print given the colour combinations."

Bickerton looking at a butterfly takes centre stage in the print of the same name (below right). "He caught sight of it in the garden; it was a surprise as we didn't know what we had until later!" The woodcut is in black ink, with the butterfly coloured with chine-collé.

Chester (below left) was a Jack Russell that Gill looked after for a while. "He loved to get comfy on the sofa, especially with his favourite cushion for extra comfort. This print is a woodcut and has three layers of ink."

The drypoint etchings 'Dog Encounters' (opposite, right) are of dogs Gill has seen on her travels. "I took photographs and sketches, then progressed to the final prints."

www.gillbedson.co.uk

NICOLA SLATTERY

While painting highly imaginative scenes often involving people and animals represents the bulk of Nicola's output, she has practised and taught printmaking techniques for many years – her perspex-based drypoints are particularly effective. A dog lover herself, she is more than happy to feature canine subjects in her works, such as the drypoints and collagraph reproduced here.

Her methods result in small hand-made editions of prints in which each image is unique. Editions are rarely of more than 12 prints due to the ephemeral nature of the plate used to create the print.

Elected to membership of the Royal Society of British Artists (RBA) in 2015, Nicola's striking work is in public, private and corporate collections around the world. She has also won numerous awards, including the Dry Red Press Award for her painting 'Songbirds', included in the 300th RBA exhibition at the Mall Galleries, London, in 2017.

www.nicolaslattery.com

From top left, clockwise: Woman with Dog (drypoint); Moon Rising (collagraph); Follow the Dog (drypoint).

A graduate of Edinburgh College of Art, Rosamund worked as a freelance illustrator for more than two decades and also produced large-scale oil paintings. In recent years she has specialised in printmaking, particularly wood engraving, and is now an elected member of the Society Of Wood Engravers.

Based in the South Downs, she is also a member of The Sussex Guild (designer-makers of contemporary and traditional crafts), with whom she regularly exhibits toy dog engravings.

One of these works, 'Frou-Frou, Fetch!' (top right) is reproduced here – the only artificial dog in the book! "Although my 'real' dog prints are of imaginary terriers [such as the Fox Terrier below right], these toy dogs on wheels actually exist, so these are portraits of some of my vintage toy collection."

'Scottie Dogs, Gullane Beach' (below left) shows two Scottish Terriers playing in the sand dunes on this beautiful East Lothian beach.

www.rosamundfowler.co.uk

ROSAMUND FOWLER

Right: Scottie Dogs, Gullane Beach.
Top right: Frou-Frou, Fetch!
Far right: Fox Terrier (all wood engravings).

JULIA MANNING

Among many awards won by versatile printmaker Julia is the first Mascot Media-sponsored 'Nature in Print' prize presented at the 2018 Society of Wildlife Artists exhibition in London. Her work combines flora, fauna and landscape to startling effect, and Julia has featured in a number of our earlier printmaking collections. Dogs may not be a speciality, but she has etched a few charming examples – including her rescue Whippet (of sorts!) Pearl.

Julia, who studied Fine Art at Bath Academy of Art, earned her living with a paintbrush for more than 30 years but now focuses on printmaking, translating her observations of nature into original prints. She uses a variety of relief and intaglio techniques, often intermixed. "Predominantly printing on to Somerset or Japanese printmaking papers, my passion for printmaking is as much about these physical processes and the craft as it is about the art.

"I am often found near my Somerset studio with binoculars or telescope in hand, watching scenarios and interactions between birds and animals," she says. "I really enjoy drawing and painting with watercolour in my sketchbooks, which I later re-interpret in printmaking. I am also passionate about colour, which I hope brings vibrancy to everything I do."

Julia is a fellow of the Royal Society of Painter-Printmakers (RE) and a member of the Society of Wildlife Artists. She is also a member of the Devon Guild of Craftsmen and of Somerset Printmakers. Her prints are in the collections of the British Embassy in Paris, Paintings in Hospitals, the Aberystwyth Print Archives, the British Museum and the House of Lords.

www.juliamanning.co.uk

Top left: Dancing Whippets.
Far left: Double Trouble OAP.
Left: Sorry (all etchings).

CHARLOTTE MATTHEWS

Charlotte, who lives and works in the Downland village of Jevington in East Sussex, takes inspiration from her surroundings and enjoys placing dogs in natural settings.

"I was raised with Lurchers, so I suppose it was inevitable that the first dog to enter my adult life should be a Lurcher. Bronte came to us through a Scottish rescue centre. She had been found tied up, and one of her legs was broken. Over the years we enjoyed many adventurous walks together, often exploring the remoter parts of Britain while camping, the three of us crammed into a two-man tent. Bronte loved it all and took life in her stride. Intelligent and easy-going, she really was the perfect canine companion.

"Inspired by the simple beauty of medieval tiles, my print 'In her Dreams' [top] shows Bronte sleeping contentedly surrounded by creatures she has encountered on her walks through the Sussex landscape.

"The materials used to create this 3-block print were readily available and cheap. I used a scalpel to make cut-outs from an old cereal box which were then glued firmly to a square of mount board. This formed the key block while two blocks of card and torn paper provided background texture. The blocks were varnished before rolling up with oil-based inks.

"Our handsome Greyhound/Saluki, Joe, was the ideal subject for 'Long Dog' [below]. He fitted nicely into this medieval-style print, being the sort of highly prized hound often seen in old tapestries and on coats of arms.

"Joe came crashing into our lives as an awkward and lively 'sapling' at around 18 months old. He was found by a friend on her way to work one autumn morning, asleep on a farm muck heap. We soon found out that he had been running loose on the South Downs, probably abandoned. A very nervous dog and wary of people, it took him many months to trust us fully. His settling-in process was greatly helped by Bronte. She was a calming influence and the perfect role model in helping him to adjust to a comfortable new home life.

"The block was cut in Asian plywood using a sharp scalpel and fine linocutting tools, and printed with oil-based inks."

Charlotte is a member of Lewes Printmakers, who meet once a week to work on both individual and group projects.
www.charlottematthews.co.uk

Top right: In Her Dreams (card relief print). Right: Long Dog (woodcut).

CLARE O HAGAN

Clare, an Irish-born visual artist and filmmaker who now lives and works in London, creates large, ambitious art projects "that convey complex aspects of the human condition". She utilises a range of media, include prints, assemblage, textiles, photography and moving image. Her favoured printmaking processes include relief, wood and lino, screenprint, lithography and aquatint.

While at work and at leisure, Clare enjoys "constant canine companionship when possible", she says. 'Sweet Shepherd' (top left) features a German Shepherd who was the star of the show at a Fun Dog Day in Derbyshire. "Stately, strong and athletic, he looked like a film star. However, in common with most dogs, he would have done a double somersault for a treat!"

Clare made 'Found Border' (top right) after finding a little Border Terrier wandering on its own in a London park. "I took it home with me; and, with the help of a friend who is a Border Terrier owner and does rescue work with the breed, it was reunited with its owner. Since then, I have been very fortunate in finding a community of dog lovers who love the breed, and now have a little Border myself."

'Blue Dalmatian' (left) "immortalises a dog named Blue who nearly killed me when I looked after her for a week!" She was a young pup, who jumped like a gazelle, from the floor to the table, to the mantelpiece on to the sofa – and my stomach! Like most pups,

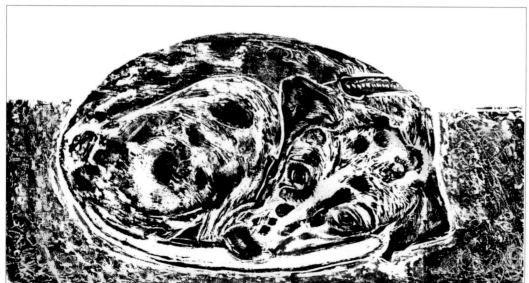

Top left: Sweet Shepherd (woodcut).
Top right: Found Border (linocut).
Left: Blue Dalmatian (woodcut).

she crashed around like a lunatic and then lay flat out for an hour. During her downtime I did some drawings, and from them made this print."

'Bordeaux Beauty' (right) features a "beautiful Dogue de Bordeaux, Will I Am, who belonged to a good friend who commissioned the print. Will I Am had such an expressive face and calm nature – a real beauty. Not long after the print was completed, Will I Am died suddenly at a very young age. His owner was so pleased to have this print as a memento of her beloved dog."

Clare created the woodcut 'Party Poodle' (below left) after meeting her at a dog show. "I was struck by the tied-up topknots and bows in her hair. Even with her hair in 'sorta' rollers, she looked elegant and assured, a real showstopper. Having looked after Poodles, I know that they are not just all show – they are very intelligent and active dogs."

Finally, 'Makhmal The Magnificent' (below right) is an Old English Bulldog whom Clare looked after regularly as a pup. "His owner was due to relocate to New York, and I was distraught to think I'd never see him again. I had absolutely fallen in love with this dog, and imagined us both running away together, or me travelling with Makhmal to the USA and getting an apartment next door to him. I made this print so that I would always have him with me, and that settled me down."

www.wyllieohagan.com

Top right: Bordeaux Beauty. Right: Party Poodle. Far right: Makhmal The Magnificent (all woodcuts).

LUCY GELL

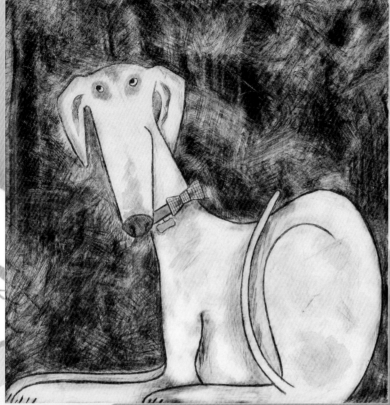

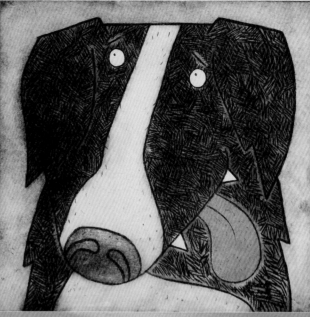

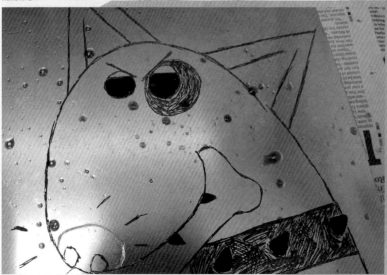

Clockwise from top left: Lurcher (drypoint); Man's Best Friend (acid etching); Fetch (acid etching); plate created as part of the printmaking process.

While working as a puppet animator, Lucy took a course in printmaking "as I felt the need to continue with illustration (in which I did my degree) – and get my hands dirty. I love the different personalities I see in animals, and this is a crucial part of the prints I create.

"When I was a child we owned many dogs with different characters and personalities. I now have the pleasure of owning a beautiful blue Whippet called Betsy and a lovely Spanish rescue Podenco called Guapa (which means 'beautiful' in Spanish). Betsy has featured in my work on many occasions, and Guapa has the perfect appearance for a caricatured dog image in my own graphic style.

"I have become very involved with the plight of the Podenco since adopting Guapa in 2018. These beautiful dogs are bred for hunting in rural areas of Spain and the Canary Islands. They have the sweetest, gentlest natures, and endure difficult lives at the hands of their owners. Many of these dogs have now found better homes in other countries.

"Giving my images character is a really important part of what I do as a printmaker and illustrator. I want my images to create a reaction from the onlooker. A character people can relate to. An image of a dog that makes them smile, sparks a memory. It is also so much about graphic design and how the images work within the space of a page."

Background image: one stage of the printmaking process under way.
Top left: Lucy Gell printing. Top right: Dog (acid etching). Above: Lucy engaged in the etching process.

www.lucygell.com

JANET GARDNER

164

PAW PRINTS

Janet's artwork is informed by her love and knowledge of dogs, her aim being to capture the spirit, personality and essence of the animal.

"Joe was a very special dog, the one who leaves footprints on your soul. A Labradoodle keen to enjoy life – walks, agility, flyball and fun tricks – his affectionate nature also made him a perfect Pets As Therapy dog."

Janet's linocuts of Labradors (right and far left, bottom), meanwhile, highlight the solid, reliable nature of the breed in contrast to the more fun approach of the Labradoodle.

George is another adorable Labradoodle, great-nephew of Joe and, unusually, black and white. He is captured with his brothers Zuma and Logan in 'The Three Muskadoodles' (bottom, second from right). Janet prepared drawings of each boy with appropriate headgear, collaged them together, photographed the image and transferred it to a solarplate etching. "It has raised smiles, and shows that lovely happy energy of Labradoodles."

In the image of Ted below, far right, Janet has captured the lively, mischievous nature of her Cockapoo, "always ready for anything".

Janet continues to experiment with different print possibilities.

www.janetgardner.net

Facing page, top left and right: Joe plate, pencil sketch and completed solarplate etching print. Right: Ben (linocut). Bottom, from far left: Labrador (linocut); Ted (screenprint/monoprint); The Three Muskadoodles plate and sketch; The Three Muskadoodles final print (solarplate etching); Ted (relief print).

HILKE MACINTYRE

WOMAN WITH POLKA DOT SKIRT

JOHN WATSON

The protagonists of John's linocut, 'Spike and Millie, Jack Russell and Spaniel', are "devoted companions driven by our friends all the way from Edinburgh to a villa in the South of France (once owned by film star Mai Zetterling) for a holiday – as you do.

"When we arrived, the weather was atrocious – torrential rain and thunderstorms – which rather put us off using the pool. Of course, the rain didn't deter the dogs, who took turns leaping into the water one after another, putting us all to shame.

"This print was from a drawing made when the two of them were cooling off after the weather returned to normal, and was a thank-you to our friends. They loved it, and it hangs in their Edinburgh home."

www.johnwatsonlinocuts.com

CYRIL VICKERS

While retired advertising Art Director Cyril doesn't actually know the Dachshund who appears in his etching with aquatint on the right, a photographic image of the dog and its ball struck him as an excellent subject for 'Fetch!'.

Cyril is the second artist appearing in this book who has been attending printmaking classes held in Sissinghurst by Amanda Averillo (page 115). He was on the creative side of the advertising industry for 45 years and, having met Amanda at a life-drawing class, began attending her printmaking workshops in Kent. He enjoys etching and monoprinting, which he feels suit his 'graphic' style.